Understanding GEN Z Slang

By

Emily T. J

Copyright © 2024 by Emily T. Jacobs.

All rights reserved. No part of this publication may be reproduced, distributed, or transmitted in any form or by any means, including photocopying, recording, or other electronic or mechanical methods, without the prior written permission of the publisher, except in the case of brief quotations embodied in critical reviews and certain other noncommercial uses permitted by copyright law.

ISBN: 978-1-7780198-6-9 (eBook)

ISBN: 978-1-7780198-7-6 (Paperback)

Disclaimer:

The following content is a parody, created for educational and entertainment purposes only. It is a fictional representation and should not be taken as factual. This work is in no way affiliated with, endorsed by, or representative of the original source material or its creators. Any similarities to real-life events, people, Karens, or organizations are coincidental and not intended to be taken as literal interpretations. While efforts have been made to ensure accuracy, no guarantees are provided. The author does not offer legal, financial, medical, or professional advice. Consult a licensed professional before applying any information here. The author is not liable for any losses or damages resulting from the use of this document, including errors or omissions.

Co-Author and Line Editor: L. Flores.

Cover by Tim Friggs.

GEN Z Slang Edits by Sid Ranni, Jessy Kay, and Oli De Luca.

eViRa TR Publishing Limited.

"Wash your hands."
　　—A famous Gen Z Influencer.

Balance is not something you find ♥ It's something you create

I like pizza

Psst.

Hey you,

Yeah, you.

My name is Emily.

Welcome to a world where everything's always on, always changing, and somehow always feels like it's JUST out of control. Sounds familiar, right? You've probably got 17 tabs open in your brain right now—some of them you didn't even mean to open.

We're living in a time when we can LITERALLY create our own avatars, scroll through endless highlights, and curate the best version of ourselves for the world to see. But here's the thing: we're also juggling real life. You know, the stuff that doesn't always make it to the feed—the awkward moments, the mess-ups, the WHAT-AM-I-DOING-WITH-MY-LIFE vibes.

This book? It's for all of us navigating this wild ride. It's not about giving you all the answers (spoiler alert: no one has them, but me). But it is about keeping it real. It's a mix of stories, advice, laughs, and maybe even a few deep thoughts. (Just kidding, this book just explains the current slang that GEN Z use, yeah, sorry for disapointment.)

You might cringe, you might laugh, you might even feel a little called out or insulted (in the best way or the worst way, anyways, lose some weight will ya?). But stick around. Whether you're vibing at the top of your game or figuring things out as you go, this is your space to feel seen.

Ready?

Let's dig into the chaos.

Table of Contents
Understanding GEN Z Slang

Asf - Asl.	1
Alpha	2
Ate.	4
Banger.	5
Based.	6
Basic.	7
BDE	8
Bestie	9
Bestie. #2	10
BET	11
BETA	12
Big Yikes	13
Blud	14
Body Count	15
Boujee	16
Bouncing	17
Bruh.	18
Bussin	19
Bussy-Bussi	20
CAP	21
Cake / Bakery	22
Caught in 4k	23
Chad (Gigachad)	24
Clapback.	26
COOK	27
COOKED	28
Cope	29
Cringe	30
Dab	31
Dank	32
Dead	34
Delulu	35
Dope	36
Dox	37
Drip	38
E	39
ERA	41
Edgy	42
Extra	43
Fad	44
FAM	45
Fave	46
FIRE	47
FIT	48
FLEX	49
Forklift Certified	50

G	51
Ghost - Ghosting	52
Girlboss	53
Glaze	54
GOAT	55
Gucci	56
Hashtag	57
Hits Different	58
Hot Take	59
Hype	60
ICK	61
Random Sounds That You Will Never Use	62
Iykyk	63
JIT	64
Karen	65
Krunk	67
Left on Read	68
LIT	70
Living Rent Free	71
Lowkey (Highkey)	72
Main Character Syndrome	73
MID	75
Mogging	77
Netflix and Chill	78
NPC	79
Nyaa	81
Nyaa (Simplified)	82
Ohio	83
Ok Boomer	84
OOF	86
OPP	87
Out of Pocket	88
Owned.	89
Periodt	90
Pick me (Girl/Guy)	91
Pluh	92
Pookie.	93
Queen	94
Ratio	95
Red Flag	96
Rizz	97
Roasted	98
Salty	99
Savage	100
Schooled	101
Secure the Bag	102
Sheesh	103
Sigma	104

SIMP 105
Skibidi 107
Slaps 108
Slay 109
Stan 110
Snatched 111
SUS 112
Take the W/Take the L 113
TAXED 114
TEA 115
Thot 116
Touch grass 117
Tweaking 118
Unsmart. 119
UWU 120
VIBE and Vibe Check 121
Wig 122
YAAS 124
YAP 126
YEET 128
Yummers. 129
GEN Z LINGO TEST. **130**
    ANSWERS 132
Author's Notes. **133**
    Certificate of Recognition 134

Asf - Asl.

Let's keep the vibe hot and read everything out loud. First we have ASF and ASL

ASF means As F*ck and ASL means As Hell. You dig? Did you like the way I censored the word F*ck? Oh, I did it again.

Please do not, and I repeat, do not report this to my publisher. I kind of want to share my witty jokes and sell my book. I promise, I won't do it again... or will I?

(Cringe, like totally. Fudge.)

Here are three examples of ASF and ASL in that same tone:

1. LIFE'S JUST CONFUSING **ASF** SOMETIMES. Like, one minute you're vibing, and the next you're questioning your entire existence because you saw some random TikTok about how dolphins sleep with one eye open. Why do they even do that? No clue. But now you're spiraling at 2 a.m. trying to figure out how your life got to this point. And honestly? Same.

2. Uh, I forgot what kind of example I wanted to say, so skip it and look for #3.

3. You're sitting there, trying to explain your life to your friends, and you're like, "BRO, I'M TIRED ASL, AND I HAVEN'T EVEN DONE ANYTHING YET." It's that kind of tired that feels like it's embedded in your soul, like you've been running a marathon just by existing. A little dramatic? Maybe. But that post-grad, existential-crisis, too-much-Netflix fatigue? It's real.

I know what you are asking, WHY ARE THE EXAMPLES CAPITALIAZED? Well, kuz I made it easier for you to read, you old dust. No offense. Moving on.

Alpha

Who are the Alphas? You've probably asked yourself this more than once after hearing Gen Z use the slang, but no worries—I'll break it down for you.

ALPHA is the top of the social food chain, the leader of the pack, the one who isn't just vibing—they're setting the vibe for everyone else. In Gen Z slang, being an ALPHA is all about confidence, authority, and that undeniable MAIN CHARACTER ENERGY. An ALPHA is the person everyone seems to orbit around, whether they're calling the shots, steering the conversation, or just walking into a room like they own the place. ALPHA is the "I'm in charge here" mindset turned up to max volume, minus any trace of doubt.

Picture this: the ALPHA walks into the group chat and says, "WE'RE MEETING AT THIS TIME, AT THIS PLACE, BRING YOUR A-GAME." And guess what? Nobody questions it—they just fall in line. Alphas have a natural magnetism that makes people want to follow them, whether they're leading a team or just deciding where everyone's getting coffee. And if an ALPHA makes a suggestion, you better believe everyone else is nodding along like it's the best idea they've ever heard.

Of course, Gen Z has turned ALPHA into more than just a personality trait. It's practically a meme now, thanks to people who hype themselves up as ALPHAS—often a little too hard. You'll see people joking about "Alpha mentality," "Alpha grindsets," and "no days off" lifestyles, like they're motivational speakers for themselves. Let's be honest: if you're calling yourself an ALPHA 24/7, there's a solid chance you're trying way too hard. Real ALPHA energy doesn't require the constant reminder—it just IS.

And if you're reading this thinking, "YEP, I'M DEFINITELY ALPHA," hold up. True ALPHA behavior means you're secure, confident, and not out here spamming your self-declared title in every convo. Alphas don't need to prove anything; they're already running the show without even breaking a sweat. So before you start bragging about your ALPHA energy, ask yourself if it's legit—or if you're just talking a big game.

ALPHA is a vibe, not a job title. If you're stepping into that role naturally, people will notice without you having to say a word.

Just remember: if you're trying to convince everyone you're an ALPHA, you might just be outing yourself as a BETA.

Sorry, not sorry. Ok, sorry. (not.)

Ate.

Ate is a bit complicated, but not as complicated as yo mama. Just kidding, don't get yikes now.

Let me bounce the wiki real quick.

So yeah, Ate is not past form of the word eat, but it kinda is, and it all depends on the context.

You spent two hours getting ready, makeup on point, fit looking fresh, and the selfies are hitting just RIGHT. You step out and, boom, YOU ATE. People are looking, and you just know you're killing it without even trying. Confidence on a hundred. It's one of those rare moments where everything just clicks, and honestly?

Go off.

If you didn't get that, it's ok. We are all dumb in our own ways. ATE is a phrase used to show admiration or praise for someone who succeeded or performed well in something. Here is another example. Read it carefully, or don't, I am a book not yo mama.

Beyoncé walks on stage? She ATE every time. When you clap back with the perfect roast in a group chat? You ATE.

Now that you got it, let's get down to B...

Banger.

A BANGER is a term used to describe a song or piece of content that absolutely slaps. We're talking about the kind of track that makes you want to turn up the volume, dance like no one's watching, and maybe even embarrass yourself a little at a party. If it's a banger, it's got that infectious energy that makes it impossible to resist singing along (even if you can't carry a tune).

Still don't get it? No worries, I will explain it to you very, very slowly.

You're at a house party, and the DJ finally drops that one song you've been waiting for all night. And yes, yes, it could be one of those old remixes from the 70s, 80s, 90s, where women had long bushy hair and men wore bell bottoms. You know, those long jeans with loose bottoms. Anyways, where were we? Oh yes, BANGER.

The whole room goes wild—people are dancing, the energy's lit, and you're thinking, "THIS IS A BANGER!" The kind of track that hits so hard, everyone forgets their awkward small talk and just vibes out.

But hold on, let's break it down: BANGER doesn't mean you're out here banging on stuff. In Gen Z world, it's when something is SO good that it gets universal approval. A song? BANGER. A movie? BANGER. Your grandma's holiday cookies? Low-key, BANGERS. Basically, if it slaps, if it's fire, it's a BANGER.

Term BANGER is used to describe something that is exceptional, impressive, or of high quality. Often referring to a catchy or energetic piece of music or a great scene in a movie.

And yeah, if someone says, "THIS PLAYLIST IS FULL OF BANGERS," get ready to have your eardrums blessed. BANGER = certified crowd pleaser. No skips, no duds—just pure hits, all day.

Based.

BASED is my fave Gen Z slang, like, no cap. I use it more often than the others. What does it mean? Based is a term of approval, affirmation, and confidence that's taken the internet by storm, especially among Gen Z. It's like saying, "You know what? You're doing you, and I'm here for it." It's all about embracing authenticity and unapologetically being yourself, no matter what the haters say.

So, you're in a group, and everyone's going off about their opinions on, like, literally everything—what's the best show, worst fast food, hottest conspiracy theory, Megan Fox, and other useless things that keep us entertained. Suddenly, you drop a comment that's so on-point, so brutally honest, and completely unbothered by what anyone else thinks. Silence for a second, and then someone replies, "THAT'S BASED."

BASED isn't about following trends or saying what's popular—it's about being unapologetically YOU. It's when you're standing firm in your beliefs, not caring if it's the "cool" thing to say. You're saying the truth as you see it, and no one can shake you. In other words, you're basically a legend in your own right.

Originally meaning "to be yourself and not care about how others view you", the word is now used to indicate an opinion or something that someone agrees with. It is especially common in political slang and discussions and may be used for controversial topics.

So when someone says, "THAT'S BASED," it's major props. It's like they're tipping their hat to your take, because you're out here speaking facts, not chasing clout.

TL;DR: BASED means you're keeping it real, very real, in fact, so real that you are staying true to yourself, and just not giving a damn if it's unpopular or might even get hated for it. It's like the opposite of being fake. And honestly? That's about as based as it gets. BASED.

Oh yeah, one more thing. TL;DR means "Too Long; Didn't Read," but that ain't Gen Z speak. So yeah, keep being based. You're basically a walking truth bomb.

Basic.

So, you're scrolling through your feed, and you see yet another person posing with a pumpkin spice latte, wearing Ugg boots, captioning their post, "Fall vibes." And you can't help but think, "Wow, that's so basic." You know the look: the same trendy stuff everyone's rocking—no originality, just straight-up cookie-cutter.

But what does BASIC actually mean? In Gen Z slang, basic describes someone who's all about super mainstream, cliché stuff. It's like playing it so safe that it feels like there's a default setting for life—like the pumpkin spice latte of personalities. Sure, it's not a bad thing, but it's predictable. It's used to denote those who prefer mainstream products, trends, and music.

If someone says, "That outfit is so basic," it's not exactly a compliment. It means you're blending in with the crowd instead of standing out. It's not a terrible thing, but it's not a great thing either. You're basically living that Pinterest starter pack life—if you know what that is, because I don't.

Please do not Google that.

Being BASIC can sometimes get a bad rap, but it's all in good fun. It's a light-hearted jab at people who might not be pushing the boundaries of creativity. Like, if your go-to outfit is a white t-shirt, jeans, and Converse, you might hear, "Wow, so BASIC," with a playful smirk.

You may hear the word NORMIE used instead of BASIC. That's okay. Being called a NORMIE means you're basic.

Pro Tip: Avoid being basic by mixing it up. No shade to pumpkin spice, but there's a whole world of flavors out there, and maybe Uggs aren't the only way to say, "I love fall."

Pro-Pro Tip: I even underlined this for you to keep in the back of your mind: Nobody actually cares about you standing out; everyone cares about their own look. So, it's not cool to call someone BASIC just because they blend in with the crowd. Stay on the side of peace. But if you do hear someone calling others basic, that's a hint that THEY might be basic.

Moral of the story: Basic is playing it safe, but you? You're here to break the mold. But you are still BASIC...

BDE

Oh, we are going to have a lot of fun with this one because it's filled with ENERGY. Yes, the "E"in BDE stands for Energy. The "B" stands for Big, and the "D" stands for... well, how do you shorten the name Richard? Ah yes, Dick. BDE is Big Duck Energy. I'm using the word "duck" to avoid Publisher's 18+ policy. Oh wait... I just said Dick, didn't I? Ok, ignore that, and let me proceed.

You walk into a room, and instantly, you feel it—the energy shifts. There's this one person standing in the corner, and they're not even trying. They just have that vibe, you know? You see your friend goes to someone and whisper, "Dude, they've got serious BDE." and he be like, "BASED." (Oh, how I love using one of my previous examples here, it makes me look so smart.)

You stand in the corner and think to yourself.

Wait, what's BDE? It stands for Big Dick Energy, and it's not just about anatomy. It's a vibe, a confidence that radiates from someone who knows their worth and isn't afraid to show it. It's the kind of presence that makes you think, "Wow, they could probably run a small country and still have time to chill."

When someone's got BDE, they're not loud or flashy; they're just naturally magnetic. You know those people who walk into a party, and everyone turns to look? Yup, that's BDE in action. It's like they have an invisible aura of confidence that says, "I'm here, and I own this place."

So, if you ever hear someone say, "They've got BDE," just know it's a major compliment. It means that person is exuding confidence without needing validation. And let's be real, we could all use a little more BDE in our lives!

Yeha, no more of BDE, kuz I don't want serious people to be on my a...butt. So, channel that energy, and remember: confidence is key, and BDE is the ultimate vibe!

Bestie

I've never used it, and you probably won't either, because neither of us has any friends. I mean, let's face it: if you had friends, you wouldn't be reading this book, and I wouldn't be writing it. So, we're going to skip it.

Bestie. #2

Offended?

Yes? No? Ok good. You asked for it.

Here is wikipedia's definition of BESTIE.

Short for "best friend." Sometimes used jokingly with someone one does not have any relationship to.

You happy now?

Now here is example of the slang to make you happier.

You and your friend are scrolling through memes late at night, and you both come across one that perfectly captures your friendship. You turn to them and say, "YOU'RE SUCH A BESTIE FOR SENDING THIS TO ME." Like, they just get you on a level no one else does, and it's like, how did you survive life without each other?

But let's break it down: what does BESTIE really mean? It's short for BEST FRIEND, but it's so much more than that. A BESTIE is that person who's always got your back, whether you're in a tough spot or just need someone to laugh with. They're the ones you can share your wildest secrets with, who will hype you up no matter what, and who always know just what to say (or not say) when you're feeling down.

When someone calls you their BESTIE, it's a badge of honor. It means you're part of a special club, one where loyalty, inside jokes, and spontaneous adventures are the main perks. It's not just about hanging out; it's about creating a bond that can survive anything.

So, if you've got a BESTIE, cherish them! And if you don't, well, you might want to get on that because life's too short not to have someone who'll be your ride-or-die, your meme partner, and your therapist all rolled into one.

Make sure they're rich too, so you can tell them about this book. Yes, I'm promoting it right now, and I know what you're thinking: what a shameless BASIC B-word. Well, I kind of need money too.

BET

You're hanging out with your crew, and someone challenges you to finish a whole pizza by yourself. You look at them, unbothered, and say, "BET." That's the kind of confidence you can only have when you know you can back it up—or you just really love pizza. Either way, it's on!

Do you want a wiki definition? Here it is. BET is Derived from non-slang bet (to bet on something). Originated in its current form from African-American vernacular and campus slang.

But what does BET really mean? In Gen Z lingo, BET is a way to say, "I'm down for that," or "I can totally do this." It's a statement of agreement or a challenge accepted. It's like saying, "You're on," but with a cooler vibe. So when someone throws down a challenge or makes a suggestion, and you respond with "BET," you're saying you're game and ready to roll.

And if you ever hear someone say, "BET," right after you mention your plans? It means they're totally in! Just know it can also be used sarcastically, like when your friend proposes something ridiculous, and you're like, "BET YOU CAN'T DO THAT."

So, whether you're up for a challenge or just vibing with your friends, throwing in a BET is a great way to keep things fun and lively. Just make sure you're ready to back it up—because with great power comes great responsibility, especially when pizza is involved!

I BET you can't finish this whole book, HA! But no, seriously, please do finish it. It took me seven months to write this, and now I'm going through two years of therapy from talking to Gen Z. What, did you think I was a Gen Z? Please, Gen Zs don't even know what a book is!

BETA

If you're unfamiliar with this one, let's just say you probably don't want to hear it aimed in your direction.

In Gen Z terms, being a BETA is a bit of a roast—it's the opposite of being a leader, a SIGMA (We'll get to this Gen Z slang later in the book.), or even an ALPHA.

A BETA is someone who's seen as following the pack, playing it safe, or letting others take the lead. Imagine someone who's too eager to please, doesn't want to step on anyone's toes, and, let's be real, probably apologizes when someone else bumps into them. That's BETA energy.

Now, let's be clear: just because someone is a BETA doesn't mean they're a bad person—it just means they might lack that edge or confidence to take charge. They're the kind of people who'd rather keep the peace than rock the boat, who'll go along with the group's decision even if it's a bad movie choice, and who'd rather avoid confrontation than call someone out. If SIGMA is the lone wolf, BETA is more like the friendly Labrador who just wants everyone to get along.

But, as always, the term BETA has taken on a life of its own in the world of Gen Z humor. It's become a playful insult, tossed around anytime someone's a little too agreeable or doesn't show enough backbone. Did you let your friend choose where to eat for the fifth time this week? BETA MOVE. Did you skip the gym because you were feeling tired? BETA. Did you double-check that text before sending it to avoid sounding too forward? Ultra BETA. It's all part of the meme: if you're not exuding total ALPHA or SIGMA vibes, you're getting called out as BETA.

So, next time you feel that BETA energy creeping in, maybe try throwing a little caution to the wind. Make a decision, skip the overthinking, or dare to take the lead. Just remember, BETA doesn't have to be an insult, but if someone calls you one, it might be time to take a little confidence boost. Because in the world of Gen Z, BETA is a title that's very hard to shake once it sticks.

Big Yikes

You probably haven't noticed how I used the word "yikes" at the beginning, but don't worry. It has a different meaning here.

Imagine you're minding your business, and suddenly you see something so cringe-worthy, so awkward, that you can't help but physically recoil. Maybe it's your friend trying to flirt with their crush in the comments section but missing the mark by, like, a mile. Or perhaps it's an old photo of your sibling rocking a hairstyle that should've never seen the light of day. In that moment, your brain goes into overdrive, and all you can say is, "BIG YIKES."

But what does BIG YIKES even mean? It's the way to express secondhand embarrassment or discomfort over something cringeworthy. Think of it as the verbal equivalent of cringing so hard you might just fold in on yourself. When you see something that makes you go, "Oh no, that's rough," or "Oh no, honey, no." It's the verbal equivalent of slapping your forehead and saying, "What were you thinking?" It's reserved for those moments where the cringe is so intense, it deserves an Olympic score of at least a 9.5.

Think of BIG YIKES as the friend who's always got your back but isn't afraid to call you out when you're about to make a monumental mistake. It's that feeling when you step on stage to give a speech and realize you're still in your pajamas. It's like witnessing someone trip in front of their crush—painful to watch but undeniably entertaining.

When you see something that gives you that delightful mix of embarrassment and schadenfreude (I never used that word in my life, and do not know what it means.), throw in a BIG YIKES. It's the perfect way to say, "I feel for you, but wow, this is a whole vibe." Just remember, we've all had our BIG YIKES moments, so wear it with pride!

Blud

So this is where we part ways, and I must away. Allow me to introduce you to my friend, my brother, my guardian angel—my BLUD. Yup, this was so cringe I almost puked. Actually, I did puke, but don't picture that. Instead, picture this: you're hanging out with your bros or sistas, and someone makes a hilarious joke that absolutely slays the mood. You look over at your friend and say, "Yo, blud, that was too funny!"

Super Secret note that might save your life: Girls don't usually use "sistah," and while they're okay with being called "bros," it's better to go with BLUD.

In Gen Z slang, BLUD is a term of endearment and camaraderie, like calling someone your bro, dude, or mate. It's casual, chill, and rolls off the tongue like butter. Originating from British slang, BLUD is often used among friends, regardless of gender.

It's that term you throw around when you want to show affection or camaraderie, usually in a playful way. So, if your friend spills their drink at a party and you can't help but laugh, a quick "COME ON, BLUD!" is the perfect response. It's all about that friendly teasing.

You're probably thinking, "Wow, she hasn't made a joke about me yet." Well, because you are one—a big one, BLUD. Haha, hahaha, ahahahaha. Okay, back to the topic.

BLUD is another word for a "friend" or "Bro" It is often used to describe people or animals that are out of place. But beware: if someone calls you BLUD with a serious tone, you might want to brace yourself. It's like when your mom uses your full name—suddenly, it's not a joke anymore, and you're in for a talk.

In short, BLUD is the term to show love and respect among your homies while keeping it casual. Just remember, when you throw around BLUD, you're basically declaring that you're in the inner circle of friendship, where laughter and playful roasting is supreme!

Body Count

BODY COUNT is a cheeky GEN Z term that refers to the number of sexual partners someone has had. It's a phrase that can spark a lot of curiosity, judgment, and even some awkward laughter when it comes up in conversation. Originally a term for something much more serious (think action movies), it's taken on a cheekier meaning when it comes to dating and relationships. When someone asks, "What's your body count?" they're not asking for your MMA stats—they're trying to find out how many romantic conquests you've racked up.

Imagine someone asking this question at a party. It's either their attempt at light-hearted banter, or it's a clumsy dive into your personal life. The question can come off as nosy, a little tacky, or downright cringe, depending on how you feel about sharing. It's basically Gen Z's small-talk trap: if someone's asking, they're likely nosier than your average gossip columnist, and if you're answering, you might as well brace for some unsolicited opinions.

Of course, BODY COUNT can be a bit of a flex, a way of bragging or building up a reputation. But in classic Gen Z fashion, it's often tossed around ironically, poking fun at how obsessed some people get with keeping score. So next time you hear someone mention their BODY COUNT, remember: it's usually more for the laughs and eyebrow raises than serious tally-keeping.

The term can also bring out the DRAMA. Some people treat their BODY COUNT like it's a scoreboard in a competition, while others use it to try and shame people for having a "high" count, which is SO outdated. At the end of the day, everyone's got their own life choices, and if someone's BODY COUNT becomes a topic of debate, you can always count on the ensuing chaos.

The best case is to never ask someone's body count unless they share it themselves, and even if they do, just act as if it's an acceptable number.

But you do you—I'm a nobody to be ordering you around.

Now, go on to the next slang.

Boujee

Get ready for a silly word in a sillier language, and no, I do not mean French, even though they are very similar. Again, do not report this to Amazon or the publishing house, I beg you. I love you, my French peeps; I adore your bread, culture, and men. (Women too, wink wink) But please, for the love of the birds and flowers, change your language.

Let's continue.

You walk into a restaurant and see someone sipping a fancy cocktail, wearing designer clothes, and casually scrolling through their latest luxury vacation pics, while wearing 30k diamond watch. You can't help but think, "Wow, they're so boujee."

But what does that even mean?

In Gen Z slang, BOUJEE (pronounced "boo-jee", sign, it is not French.) describes someone who has expensive tastes or a flair for the finer things in life. It's like the ultimate lifestyle flex, often accompanied by a hint of "I may or may not be pretending to be rich." If you love brunching on avocado toast with edible flowers while wearing a $200 shirt, congratulations—you're living your best boujee life!

The term originally comes from the word "bourgeois," which refers to the middle class, but let's be real—no one wants to be just "middle class." We're talking about that vibe, a fancy vibe where everything is a little extra, whether it's your coffee being served in a mason jar with a whip cream or your friend insisting on taking a private jet for a weekend getaway, even though you both are broke.

BOUJEE can also have a humorous twist. It's not always serious! If your friend insists on ordering a $10 bottled water while the rest of you are sipping on good ol' tap, you might chuckle and say, "Alright, we get it—you're boujee." It's the perfect way to poke fun at someone who's living large, even if they're really just stretching their paycheck for that designer handbag.

And yes, do get rid of that friend who buys a bottle of water for ten bucks. Like, what the actual duck? $10 for a botta of wata? Get the heck out of here!

Bouncing

This is getting serious, and no, I'm not joking this time. The Gen Z slang for "bouncing" has two meanings—one of them not so great (let's just say it involves two naked people doing a rodeo), and the other one, which I'll explain here.

So, your friend invites you to a party, but halfway through, you realize it's not really your scene. People are doing awkward TikTok dances, the music's questionable, and there's no food in sight. You glance at your phone, nudge your friend, and say, "Yo, I'm bouncing on this."

Translation: You're outta there!

In Gen Z slang, BOUNCING ON IT is a playful way of saying, "I'm leaving" or "I'm dipping out." It's used when you want to make an exit—whether from a boring situation, a conversation that's going nowhere, or a party that's just not hitting right. Basically, when you're done with something and ready to move on, you're bouncing on it.

And the best part? It sounds cooler than just saying, "I'm leaving." Why simply leave when you can bounce? It adds a little extra flair to your departure, like you're making an escape with style. Plus, it's a great way to casually exit without feeling awkward.

It's not just limited to social situations, either. Didn't vibe with a show on Netflix? Bouncing on it. Done with a conversation that's dragging on? Bouncing on it. Your boss hits you with a surprise Zoom meeting at 4:59 p.m.? Well, mentally, you're already bouncing on it.

When you're ready to make your grand (or not-so-grand) exit, just say you're BOUNCING ON IT and leave with confidence! Because sometimes, life's all about knowing when to dip out.

BOUNCE.

Bruh.

Finally. Freaking finally—my favorite word and the one I've used the most while talking to Gen Z: BRUH. And no, it doesn't mean bro or brother. Quite different. BRUH has both a positive vibe and one that says, "Really, dude?" So, it's all about the context.

According to Wikipedia (thank God for Wikipedia, otherwise I would have failed my college years and become a writer... wait a minute...), BRUH is a term used to express a feeling of shock, embarrassment, or disappointment toward something or someone. Well, its basically another word for "Really?", but not really...

You know that moment when something so wild or ridiculously unexpected happens that words just escape you? Like, your friend just told you they accidentally texted their crush the most embarrassing message imaginable, and all you can say is, "Bruh."

In Gen Z slang, BRUH is the all-purpose reaction word. It can mean "Are you serious?" or "No way!" or even just "Wow." It's the perfect thing to say when you're so shocked, confused, or dumbfounded that no other word will do. It's like a verbal eye-roll or an "I can't even" wrapped up into one syllable.

But BRUH is versatile.

Your friend just pulled a crazy stunt on their skateboard? BRUH. You just found out your favorite artist dropped a surprise album? BRUH. Your sibling ate the last slice of pizza that you were saving? Big BRUH energy. It can convey surprise, disbelief, approval, or disappointment all at once, depending on the tone. It's like the Swiss Army knife of reactions.

And let's be honest, there are big BRUH moments happening daily. Your teacher assigns a five-page essay due tomorrow? BRUH. Your phone dies at 1% right before you send an important text? BRUH. You realize you've been wearing your shirt inside out all day? Yep, BRUH.

Bussin

BUSSIN pronounced as the word BUS, just add the SIN. I know what you are thinking, please do not think that, it is not the word that you think it is, though it does sound the same. It is actually a good word, mind you.

Let me explain,

Say you're about to sit down to eat, and the moment you take that first bite, your taste buds are hit with an explosion of flavor. It's so good that you can't even find the words, so all you say is, "YO, THIS IS BUSSIN!"

In Gen Z lingo, BUSSIN is the highest form of praise, used when something—usually food—is so delicious, so fire, that you just have to give it the recognition it deserves. That burger? BUSSIN. Grandma's mac and cheese? BUSSIN. Your friend's homemade cookies? They didn't just bake, they BUSSED.

But here's the catch: BUSSIN isn't just for food!

It can be used to describe anything that's hitting all the right notes. Your new outfit? BUSSIN. That new song on your playlist? BUSSIN. Your squad's vibe at a party? You guessed it—BUSSIN. It's basically a way to say, "THIS IS TOP-TIER," like an elite stamp of approval.

Now, be warned: using BUSSIN comes with serious responsibility. Not every sandwich deserves the title, and not every meal will be BUSSIN. So, reserve it for those truly next-level experiences—because when you say something's BUSSIN, you're telling the world it's not just good, it's life-changing.

Next time you're diving into something that's 10/10, don't just say it's good—go ahead and declare it BUSSIN. Because when it's that good, you know it deserves more than a basic compliment.

Bussy-Bussi

BUSSI(Y) pronounced as Boosi. Get your mind out of the gutter, actually don't, kuz it will get worse.

Do not confuse with the word, BUSSIN, kuz they are not related and do not sound nor mean the same thing. I know a lot of older peeps keep saying this word to mean the other, but it does not and will not.

Now back to BUSSY…Boy, oh boy, here we go.

BUSSY, or a BUSSI. You might be thinking, "WHAT IN THE WORLD DOES THAT WORD EVEN MEAN…?" But bear with me—it's Gen Z slang that's a bit cheeky (pun intended)

BUSSY is a playful and humorous mashup of "BOY" OR "BUTT" and "PUSSY"—used to describe, well, a certain part of the male anatomy. The rear part of the male anatomy…basically his butt.

Specifically speaking, it's a funny way to refer to a guy's, ahem, rear end(butt, it is butt ok?) in contexts that are usually lighthearted or flirty. People throw it around when they want to inject some humor into conversations about body parts or when poking fun at sexuality and gender in a non-serious way.

If someone says "WORK THAT BUSSY" or "HE'S GOT HIS BUSSY OUT" (metaphorically, of course, or maybe not), it's all about playing with language, often in LGBTQ+ spaces where people have a blast remixing words for comedic effect. Like BUSSY, a lot of this slang is meant to be light, fun, and sometimes over-the-top ridiculous.

When you see the term BUSSY pop up, just know it's all part of Gen Z's playful, and sometimes hilariously absurd way of keeping conversations spicy. Just use it with the right crowd—you know, the one that'll laugh along!

CAP

You are still here? Oh man, you are a persistant guy or girl, I don't care, I don't see gender, I see your money. Thank you for buying my book. I love you.

Anyways.

I thought you'd given up by now, NO CAP. See what I did there? I used the word CAP as an example here, now let me explain what it means.

Let's say your friend rolls up, flexing like they've just bought a private island, a luxury yacht, and enough sneakers to fill an entire mansion. You look at them, raise an eyebrow, and say, "BRO, THAT'S CAP." Translation: You're calling them out for lying, exaggerating, or straight-up making stuff up!

In Gen Z slang, CAP means LIE or FALSEHOOD. So when someone's trying to pull a fast one on you, or just telling a wild story that you KNOW didn't happen, you throw out a quick "CAP" to set the record straight. And if you really want to drive the point home, you hit them with "BIG CAP." That's like saying, "This is the MOUNT EVEREST of lies."

The opposite of CAP? NO CAP. The one I used at the beginning of this page. That's when you're saying something true, honest, or real. Like when you tell your friend, "THIS PIZZA IS THE BEST THING I'VE EVER EATEN, NO CAP." Now they know you're not playing around; that pizza is truly bussin' (see what I did there? Ok, ok, I will stop with my witty remarks, but I do want some praise from you, *smiles happily*).

In short, when something's sus (We will get to the word "SUS" when we get to the letter S, but for now, just keep it in mind) and the truth seems a little too good to be real, just pull out CAP like a verbal buzzer. Womp womp. Because no one's got time for fake flexes!

Whenever you hear someone going off about how they could totally lift 300 pounds or claim they met Beyoncé at the grocery store, just hit them with a smooth "CAP." It's the modern, Gen Z-approved way to say, "YEAH, I'M NOT BUYING THAT."

CAKE / BAKERY

CAKE and BAKERY—two sweet little slang terms that seem harmless but are packing some serious, uh, "assets." In Gen Z lingo, when people talk about CAKE, they're not discussing dessert. They're talking about someone's behind—their booty, their backside, their...well, you get the idea. If someone's got "cake," it means they've got a well-endowed rear that's impossible to ignore. And yes, it's definitely a compliment, albeit a cheeky one (pun intended).

So, when someone says, "SHE'S GOT CAKE," they're definitely not inviting you to a party for sweets—unless you count admiring someone's curves as the "party." And if you hear, "HE'S GOT CAKE," you know exactly what they mean: that person is working with some serious glutes.

And BAKERY? Oh, that's when someone's bringing a whole lot more than just CAKE—they've got the full spread, multiple layers, a whole stockpile, if you will. It's like leveling up from a single dessert to a full-service shop. If someone's packing a BAKERY, they've got enough CAKE to keep the metaphorical pastry business booming.

When someone mentions CAKE or BAKERY, know that Gen Z isn't talking about carbs—they're paying homage to the, let's say, "well-rounded" figures around them. Just remember, keep it respectful because, well, you wouldn't want to get caught ogling the BAKERY uninvited.

Do I have cake? First of all, how DARE you ask a lady that? Second, yes, yes, I DO have cake—though, it doesn't come with much of calories.

Caught in 4k

Remember the days of 360p being an amazing quality of video resolution? Yeah, I don't either. GEN Z peeps nowdays don't even know what 480p or 720 is, but they do know what 4k is.

Let me explain.

It refers to someone being indisputably caught doing something wrong or incriminating on camera or with evidence to prove it, referencing 4K resolution.

Let me <u>example it</u>. Oh no, I am making a new slang for GEN Z? please save me...

Your friend's been talking all week about how they're sticking to their diet, but you KNOW you saw them sneak into the kitchen late at night for a whole pizza, fries, fatty sauce and a bottle of pepsi. You have the receipts—a crystal-clear video of them going to town on that cheesy goodness. You bust out your phone and say, "BRUH, YOU'RE CAUGHT IN 4K!"

Their face goes red, and they try to play it off with, "NAH, THAT'S NOT ME... THAT'S MY TWIN COUSIN." But it's too late. The fries don't lie, and neither does 4K!

In Gen Z slang, CAUGHT IN 4K means you've been exposed with undeniable, high-definition evidence. It's like saying, "WE'VE GOT THE PROOF, AND THERE'S NO WAY YOU'RE GETTING OUT OF THIS ONE." The "4K" part comes from the term for ultra-high-resolution video, implying that not only were you caught red-handed, but you were caught with such clarity that there's no wiggle room to deny it.

You were sneaking around? CAUGHT IN 4K. You said you weren't going to text your ex but then accidentally posted a screenshot of the convo? Yeah, that's CAUGHT IN 4K. It's like being caught with a security camera zooming in on you from every angle.

Basically, it's a way of saying, "We've got you, no cap (Heck yeah, I am smart)," and it's often used playfully to tease friends when they get busted doing something they didn't think anyone noticed.

Chad (Gigachad)

CHAD and GIGACHAD are the compliments (or sometimes roasts) in internet culture. A CHAD is the stereotypical "alpha" guy who's effortlessly confident, admired, and somehow always winning at life. But GIGACHAD? That's a CHAD on steroids—he's basically evolved into a next-level, almost mythical creature who does everything better, faster, and cooler than anyone else. If there were a Hall of Fame for being iconic and outrageously self-assured, the GIGACHAD would be its eternal ruler.

Imagine someone who walks into a room and instantly commands attention, like they're the main character and everyone else is just an extra. The CHAD is the kind of person who doesn't need validation—they're already convinced of their greatness, and they've probably been told they're right a few too many times. Now, GIGACHAD takes it further. He's got the confidence of a lion, the jawline that could chisel granite, and the life skills of someone who's never failed a day in his life. If the GIGACHAD were to apply for a job, he'd probably get hired AND end up as the CEO by the end of the week.

In meme culture, GIGACHAD is typically used in a funny, exaggerated way, making him an icon of absolute superiority—he's always doing things at 200% while everyone else struggles at a measly 50%. If you manage to lift a heavy box, GIGACHAD has already lifted a car. If you tell a good joke, GIGACHAD has a comedy special.

On the flip side, calling someone a CHAD or GIGACHAD can also be a way of poking fun. Like if your friend gets an A on a test without studying or walks out of the gym like they own the place, you might tease, "Alright, GIGACHAD, save some glory for the rest of us." It's that mix of admiration and gentle mockery that makes it perfect for lighthearted teasing.

Whether you're a CHAD doing your best or a full-on GIGACHAD who just can't stop winning, embrace the title with pride (or maybe a little humility for everyone else's sake)! Just remember, there's always a bit of irony in the GIGACHAD status—it's part admiration, part over-the-top fun, and all in good humor.

Take a break and drink some water.

You are welcome.

:)

Clapback.

You're minding your business, posting a fire selfie on Instagram, when suddenly, someone leaves a comment like, "TOO BAD YOU DON'T HAVE A PERSONALITY TO MATCH."

Yikes!

But instead of letting it slide, you hit them with the comeback: "I'D AGREE, BUT YOU'D NEED A PERSONALITY TO RECOGNIZE ONE." Boom—CLAPBACK achieved.

In Gen Z slang, a CLAPBACK is a sharp, witty, and often savage response to someone's rude comment or insult. It's not just any reply; it's a comeback so on point that it leaves the other person speechless, rethinking their whole life. The goal of a CLAPBACK? To defend yourself with style, humor, and maybe a little spice. It's all about turning the tables and making the original comment seem weak in comparison. A Swift and witty response to an insult or critique.

The best CLAPBACKS are quick and effortless—like you've been preparing for this moment your entire life. Someone says, "WOW, YOU LOOK TIRED," and you hit them with, "YEAH, FROM CARRYING THIS CONVERSATION." That's peak CLAPBACK energy.

And the beauty of a CLAPBACK? It's not just about shutting someone down—it's about doing it with finesse. You're not just roasting them, you're serving them a five-course meal of sarcasm with a side of EXTRA.

When someone comes for you, don't just let it slide. Hit them with a CLAPBACK so good, they'll think twice before trying you again. Just remember, when you clap back, make sure it's HOT(Insert "Fire" emoji) enough to leave them reeling—but still classy enough to keep it fun!

COOK

Hehehe, alright, we have finally reached the most used word after BASED, BET and BRUH. The COOK.

Imagine this: you're hanging out with your crew, and someone just absolutely DESTROYS a dance move at the party. They hit every beat, every step, and the crowd is going wild. You lean over to your friend, eyes wide, and say, "BRO, THEY'RE COOKING!"

In Gen Z slang, COOK means someone is absolutely KILLING IT—whether it's on the dance floor, during a performance, or even in a heated debate. When you say someone is "cooking," you're saying they're in the zone, performing at their absolute best, and nobody can touch them.

It's like watching someone drop 50 points in a basketball game while everyone else is just trying to keep up. Or when your friend is on fire during a game of CALL OF DUTY, racking up kills like they're on a mission, you hit them with, "YO, YOU'RE COOKING, MY GUY!"

And it doesn't stop at sports or gaming. If someone delivers a hilarious roast in a group chat or gives a presentation that leaves everyone stunned, you could be like, "THEY COOKED." It's the perfect compliment for anyone absolutely NAILING it.

Next time someone is on fire, whether they're dancing, gaming, or just straight-up owning the moment, tell them they're COOKING. Because when someone's that good, you know they're serving up more than just heat—they're in chef mode, no cap!

COOKED

Yup, that is right. If there is a COOK, there is a COOKED. That sentence made no freaking sense whatsoever, but you got the point, kuz by now you should have lost your mind and your brain became a GEN Z like thinking machine.

You know that feeling when it's been a LONG day, and you're mentally and physically DONE, like done-done, like you've just run a marathon, solved quantum physics, listened to your aunt nagging for 6 hours, and been through an emotional rollercoaster all in the span of 24 hours? That's when you're officially COOKED.

In GEN Z, COOKED means you're completely exhausted, overwhelmed, or just utterly defeated by whatever life's thrown at you. It's like saying, "I'M FRIED, I'M DONE, I'M BEYOND REPAIR." You've hit that point where your brain has turned to mush, and your energy levels are in the negatives.

Example: You just pulled an all-nighter studying for an exam, only to realize that none of the material you crammed for is on the test. Afterward, you stare at the exam paper, utterly defeated, and say to your friend, "BRO, I'M COOKED."

But COOKED doesn't just apply to mental exhaustion. It's also used when someone has seriously messed up or gotten WRECKED. Like, if your friend just got roasted in the group chat and didn't even have a comeback, you might say, "DUDE, YOU GOT COOKED!" It's the verbal version of saying, "YOU'RE TOAST."

Whether you're completely drained from a long day or just got owned in a debate, COOKED is the perfect way to express that you're done—like, stick a fork in me, I'm COOKED.

Cope

In Gen Z slang, COPE is what you say when someone is struggling to accept reality, especially when that reality isn't in their favor. If someone's whining, making excuses, or just plain delusional about something that didn't go their way, Gen Z has one thing to say: COPE. It's basically the modern way of saying, "You bought this book. Deal with it" or "You don't like the author? Cry about it," but with a little extra salt thrown in for flavor.

Imagine this: your friend just got demolished in an online debate but insists they actually won because of some obscure technicality. Your response? "COPE." Or maybe someone's ranting about how they TOTALLY could have made the team if the coach "didn't have it out for them." Mmm...COPE. It's like a quick, one-word reality check—sometimes compassionate, but mostly not.

COPE is also often used in meme culture as a way to mock people who can't handle hearing something they don't like. Picture someone in denial, spinning excuses left and right to make themselves feel better. They're desperately searching for reasons they're actually right or why it's not THEIR fault. And you? You're sitting back with a smirk, muttering, "COPE." The word suggests they should just accept the truth and move on rather than fight a losing battle.

If you find yourself on the receiving end of COPE, maybe it's time to reconsider the situation. Or, if you're the one dishing it out, savor the moment. Because COPE is about as close as you can get to a verbal eye-roll, letting people know they're wasting their time fighting the inevitable. #Cope. (I'll explain the # in a few pages, so bear with me.)

Cringe

Cringe is short for "cringeworthy." But do you really think Gen Z is going to spell out the whole word for you? Nah, they'd rather watch fifteen TikTok posts than waste time typing out six extra letters.

CRINGE is the word for those moments that are so awkward, embarrassing, or painfully try-hard that you can practically feel your soul leaving your body out of secondhand embarrassment. If something is CRINGE, it's trying way too hard and missing the mark by a mile—and you can't look away, even if you want to. It's like a social trainwreck where everyone is quietly horrified but also morbidly entertained.

Imagine someone delivering an over-the-top pickup line at a party, winking way too hard and smirking like they're the hottest thing on two legs. You're left staring, half in shock and half in pity, thinking, "That was so CRINGE." Or maybe your high school principal starts using TikTok slang to connect with "the youths," and you're just begging them to stop before you burst into flames from embarrassment. It's that moment when someone's trying to be funny, relatable, or cool, and they're hitting every wrong note possible.

CRINGE has even become its own genre of internet content, where people post mortifying fails, disastrous pickup attempts, or painfully staged "epic" moments. Whether it's someone singing out of tune on a talent show with absolute confidence or trying to look tough but tripping over their own feet, CRINGE content is like a car crash—you feel bad, but you also can't look away.

It's also a way to check people when they're doing something over-the-top and unnecessary. If someone keeps making dramatic, heartfelt speeches every time they get an "achievement unlocked" in a game, you might side-eye them and say, "Alright, we get it, no need to be CRINGE."

But here's the kicker: sometimes the CRINGE is what makes life hilarious. We all have our CRINGE moments, and, if anything, it just means we're human. Embrace it (at least a little) because if you can't laugh at your own CRINGE, who can? Just remember, there's a fine line between being confidently yourself and diving headfirst into CRINGE territory.

Dab

I am blue, da ba dee da ba di. Da ba dee da ba di, da ba dee da ba di. Da ba dee da ba di, da ba dee da ba di. Da ba dee da ba di, da ba dee da ba di. I am blue, da ba dee da ba di. Da ba dee da ba di, da ba dee da ba di. Da ba dee da ba di, da ba dee da ba di. Da ba dee da ba di, da ba dee da ba di. God, I love this song when I was a teenager. I used to listen to it for hours. GEN Z of today will never know the struggle of finding the right music in the MTV channel.

Ok, back on track.

The word DAB is never part of the song's lyrics, even though it is a dance move. And it is not just a dance move. it is a legendary dance move that involves dropping your head into the crook of one arm while extending the other arm out straight. It's quick, it's simple, and for a brief moment, it was the ULTIMATE way to flex on your success. It became popular around 2015-2016, often associated with victory, hype moments, or just goofing around.

In Gen Z culture, the DAB was everywhere—from sports celebrations to memes to even your teacher trying (and usually failing) to stay hip by dabbing in class. It became a symbol of triumph, like the modern-day equivalent of a victory lap. Got a good grade on your test? DAB. Pulled off the perfect prank on your friend? DAB. Managed to make it through a full Monday without napping? Major DAB energy.

But let's be real: The DAB has since hit "retirement" status. Some kids still use it, but only for the vibes and trends, nothing more and nothing less.

It's now less of a hype move and more of a relic from a few years ago—so much so that pulling out a dab today might get you some playful eye-rolls or groans. That's what makes it FUNNY though—doing it ironically is half the charm now. Hit a dab at just the right (or wrong) moment, and you've got instant comedy.

While the DAB may have faded from its peak, don't sleep on it! It's still perfect for that nostalgic, over-the-top celebration. Just hit that DAB, and let the cringey glory unfold.

Dank

I 100% guarantee that you've probably heard a phrase like "That's a dank meme, yo" or "Bruh, that move was dank," and you were probably wondering, *I only got some words out of that sentence. What the heck does DANK mean?* Well, I'm here to explain.

DANK is the go-to Gen Z word for something that's not just good, but weirdly and unexpectedly great. Think of it as the internet's high praise for things that are oddly satisfying, a little edgy, or just too funny to be ignored. If you see someone sharing "dank memes," expect the kind of humor that's either hilariously random or teetering on the edge of what's socially acceptable (or both). It's like saying, "This is so offbeat, it's genius."

When someone says something is DANK, they mean it's not just cool; it's oddly, inexplicably, "why-do-I-love-this?" cool. Imagine finding a meme that's borderline nonsense but leaves you laughing so hard you spill your overpriced oat milk latte. That's DANK—it's like a special stamp of approval for things that are so offbeat you need a personality quiz just to get them.

You might use DANK to describe things that are surprisingly amazing despite their oddness, like a weird new show that's unexpectedly addicting or a food combination that shouldn't work but DOES. Or, it might be that your friend finally showed you their playlist of underground artists that have that "this slaps but why?" vibe. That's DANK.

Originally, DANK described something damp and musty, so how did it go from "questionable basement smell" to "certified cool"? It's the ultimate glow-up, capturing the vibe of something that's not conventionally perfect but hits differently in the best possible way. And it's not just reserved for memes—any oddly satisfying or meme-worthy experience can be DANK.

And when it comes to DANK MEMES, it's the DEEP CUTS of the meme world—the type of stuff that'd make your grandma cry from confusion. But hey, you'll laugh so hard that you'll forget how close it hit to home. You might even start calling yourself DANK, which is like telling the world you're a strange masterpiece in progress, and they can either keep up or get left behind. So, next time someone tells you something you like is

DANK, take it as both a compliment and a reminder: you're a weirdo... but in a very exclusive club.

Dead

I wish GEN Z would create new words such as BRUH or BLUD, but no, sometimes they use the existing word but change the meaning of it. For example, the word DEAD. A normal functioning adult that provides for society would recognize the word DEAD and think that it means death or gone. But nooooooooooooo, in GEN Z lingo, it means...to describe something humorous. Yup, you read that right. Dead is now an explanation that something is so funny it might kill you. Aside from UNALIVE and LYKYK, this is one of those words you will be using lot of times.

You still don't get it? Its alright. That is why I wrote this book with detailed explanations for people like us...that need to concentrate on the new trends.

Alright, imagine you're scrolling through TikTok, and you come across a video of someone absolutely butchering a dance move, tripping over their own feet, and face-planting into the floor. You're laughing so hard that you can barely breathe, tears in your eyes. What do you do? You type "I'M DEAD" in the comments. Why? Because the video was so funny, you feel like you've DIED from laughter.

In Gen Z slang, DEAD is used to describe something so hilarious or outrageous that it figuratively "kills" you with laughter. It's like saying, "I'M LAUGHING SO HARD, I CAN'T EVEN DEAL!" No actual death involved, just pure comedic annihilation. You might also see "I'M DECEASED," "I'M IN THE GRAVE," or "I'M DONE"—all of which mean the same thing: something was ridiculously funny or too much to handle.

DEAD isn't just limited to humor, though. It can also apply when you're absolutely shocked or shook by something—like when your friend tells you they just saw someone wear Crocs to a wedding, and you're like, "I'M DEAD. THAT'S TOO MUCH."

The next time you see something that's so funny it knocks the life out of you (in the best way possible), just hit them with, "I'M DEAD." Because sometimes, when words fail, laughter kills... and it's a vibe.

Delulu

Can you imagine that the Gen Z peeps don't know how to spell DELUSIONAL? Yup, that's right. They don't, and that's why they created the word DELULU. But wait, in their defense, DELULU is mostly (but not always) used in the context of relationships. Like I said, not always, but mostly. Pay attention.

Let's say your friend is completely convinced that their crush, who barely knows they exist, is secretly in love with them because "they liked my Instagram story once." Meanwhile, everyone else is looking at them like, "Bruh, you're straight-up delusional." But in Gen Z slang, we just say, "You're DELULU."

DELULU is short for DELUSIONAL, and it's used when someone's thoughts or beliefs are way out there—like in a whole different dimension of reality.

It's not just being a little optimistic or hopeful; it's when someone is so convinced of something ridiculous or unrealistic that you can't help but shake your head and say, "You're so DELULU."

For example, your friend thinks they're going to become a millionaire by next week because they bought one lottery ticket, or they watched some random youtuber explaining how to get rich within 48 hours. THEY ARE DELULU. They think their favorite celebrity noticed their comment in a sea of 10,000? Big DELULU energy. It's all about poking fun at those wild, over-the-top fantasies that everyone knows are a bit too far-fetched.

But here's the thing—being DELULU can actually be kind of fun. Sometimes, it's just about letting yourself dream big or believe in wild possibilities, even if they're totally unrealistic. Because who knows? Maybe one day, the universe will surprise you. Or maybe you'll just stay DELULU, and that's fine too.

Dope

Alright, brace yourself, because we're about to talk about a word so cool, so effortlessly "in," that you're probably not ready for it. Yes, I'm talking about DOPE. Now, if you're sitting there thinking, "WAIT, ISN'T THAT A 90S WORD?" first of all—WOW. How did you end up with this book in your hands? Did you just roll out from under a rock or something?

Let's break it down

DOPE is the word to describe something seriously impressive or amazing. It's like the "hey, look at me, I'm too cool to use 'cool'" of words. When you call something dope, you're saying it's top-tier, next-level. That concert you just went to? Dope. Your friend's new shoes? Dope.

This book you're reading? Obviously DOPE. And if you disagree, kindly return the book to the Amazon/Store. (I'm sorry. Please don't return it—I need the money. Also, leave a review. Me love you long time.)

Using DOPE correctly could almost—ALMOST—make you sound like you have some grasp on current slang. But let's not get carried away here. Just because you've mastered DOPE doesn't mean you're ready to roll with Gen Z. You've got a long way to go, my friend, and I'm not even sure you're up for it. But hey, I won't tell your cooler, younger acquaintances you're secretly brushing up on their lingo.

DOPE might sound effortless, but let's be real—DOPE isn't for the faint-hearted or the mediocre. No one's calling your Monday meeting DOPE unless you work at a donut shop and your boss brings fresh cronuts every day. DOPE is reserved for moments and things that stand out, like your friend's ridiculous guitar solo, a next-level outfit, or maybe even that one time you managed not to spill your coffee while running late. (Rare, but definitely DOPE.)

And if someone calls you DOPE, congrats, you're officially in the big leagues of cool. You've surpassed mere "not bad" status and achieved something worth a standing ovation—or at least a head nod from across the room. Just don't go throwing around DOPE for anything and everything, or it'll lose its edge, and then what will you have left? "Nice"? Nah, DOPE is too good for that.

Dox

I'm so glad I lived my childhood in the era of no social media, because the amount of stupid things I did and said would be all over the internet. Sadly, in today's world, where everyone has a cellphone and everything can be easily recorded, one must always be careful about how they act and what they say.

I am clean—well, at least I WAS clean before I wrote this book...

Now, what does DOX actually mean?

DOX is the act of digging up and publicly sharing someone's personal information online without their consent, usually to expose or embarrass them. When someone gets DOXED, it means details like their address, phone number, or even workplace have been broadcasted for all to see, often as a revenge tactic or a way to make a serious online beef painfully real. It's the internet's version of flipping over the Monopoly board—but instead of just game pieces flying, it's your whole identity.

Here's how DOXING usually goes down: someone online gets into a heated argument, decides they're done with the usual back-and-forth, and suddenly, they're Sherlock Holmes on a caffeine high. Next thing you know, they're posting the other person's details like they're unveiling a scandal on prime-time TV. If that sounds intense, it's because it is—and also wildly unnecessary. DOXING is like the nuclear option of internet arguments; it's not just overkill, it's completely out of bounds.

Being DOXED is no joke—it's like getting caught by the entire internet with your digital pants down, and there's really no coming back from it unscathed. So, next time you're feeling petty online, remember: it's best to keep things chill and keep everyone's private details where they belong—private. Save the doxing energy for something productive, like figuring out how to finally beat that hard level in Candy Crush.

Drip

How do you spot a Gen Z freelancer? They're the ones asking for Wi-Fi at the coffee shop. I hope no GEN Z reads my book, or I will be in so much trouble (or cringe, yeah, more like cringe, they will never find a report button nor read a book).

Back to the example,

You're walking down the street, and someone passes by looking SO fresh that you almost stop in your tracks. They've got the perfect fit—designer shoes, a clean jacket, chains glistening in the sunlight. You're thinking, "WOW, THEY'VE GOT MAD DRIP, YA-YO." Ignore the YA-YO part, in my 7 months of research I only heard one GEN Z say that, and he got punched for it.

In Gen Z lingo, DRIP refers to someone's impeccable, stylish, and often expensive outfit or appearance. If you've got DRIP, you're not just wearing clothes—you're making a statement. You're flexing your fashion game so hard that people can't help but notice. It's like your outfit is so on point that it's DRIPPING with swag.

You don't just wear DRIP; you OWN it. Whether it's your shoes, your jewelry, or the way you coordinate everything down to your socks, it's all about looking like a million bucks—even if you're just running to the grocery store. Got a fresh pair of Jordans? That's DRIP. Rocking a custom leather jacket with gold chains? You're dripping so hard, it's a flood.

But DRIP isn't just about high fashion. It's about CONFIDENCE. You could be wearing thrift store finds, but if you're wearing them with swagger and making people stop and take note? That's still DRIP. It's all in how you carry yourself.

Next time you see someone looking like they just stepped out of a fashion magazine, go ahead and say, "YOUR DRIP IS FIRE!" Because if you've got the drip, you're already winning—no cap!

E

E. Just the single letter. One vowel. One simple, open-mouthed sound. Yet it has so much potential to throw people off. **E** is the chaotic, meme-fueled shorthand that embodies everything about Gen Z's love for randomness. It's a letter that started making waves thanks to internet culture and an obsession with absurdity that only the true memelords understand.

Where did **E** come from? **E** became legendary through one iconic meme where Markiplier's face is Photoshopped onto Lord Farquaad's body from SHREK, with just a giant, unexplained "E" slapped across the screen. Yes, it makes zero sense. No, you don't need to get it—that's the point. **E** is peak Gen Z humor: it's weird, it's pointless, and it doesn't need a deeper meaning.

It's just FUNNY because... why not?

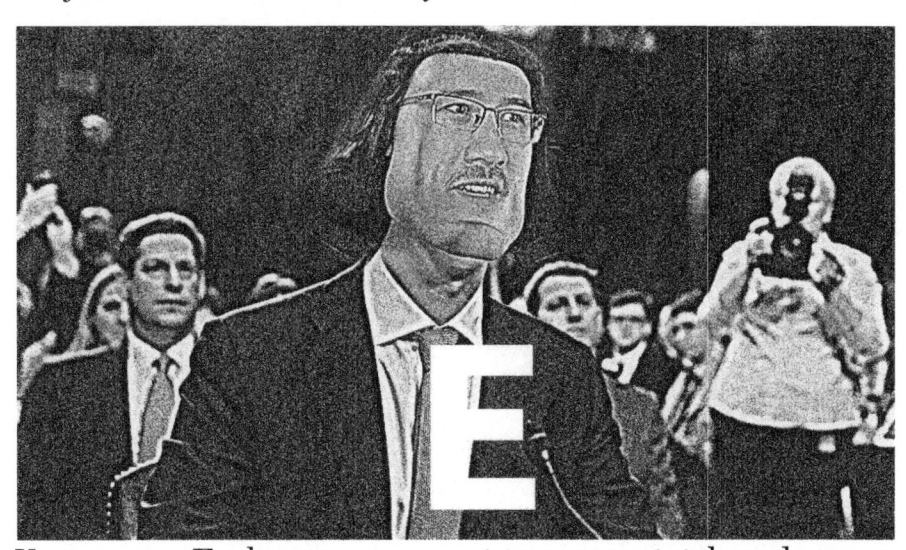

You can use **E** whenever you want to express total randomness, surprise, or even to troll someone who's expecting a more logical response. Imagine someone texts you with a long, heartfelt message, and your only response is E. It's like the ultimate troll move. Your friend tells you about their relationship drama? E. Someone asks you what you're doing later? **E**. There is no context, and there's no need for it.

This is where Gen Z thrives—**E** is here to throw logic out the window and let absurdity reign supreme. Just lean into the confusion. And next time you want to make someone question their understanding of reality, hit them with a solid **E**. If they get it, they get it. If they don't? Well... they'll just have to BECOME part of the meme.

E.

Funny, isn't it? Are you laughing? Please, tell me you're laughing. Let me try that one more time.

E.

ERA

Okay, I hope you've calmed down after laughing so much... Now, we move on to ERA. You've probably heard people talking about being in their "GYM ERA", or "STUDYING ERA", or even their "SELF-CARE ERA". And let's be real—you're probably in your "PROCRASTINATION ERA" right now, aren't you? No shame, we've all been there. (Do your work, shame on you.)

In Gen Z slang, ERA is a term used to define a specific phase or period someone's going through, like it's a whole chapter of their life. It's like branding your current vibe, habits, or obsession as a defining moment. But don't get it twisted—it's not some deep, philosophical life journey. You're not Gandhi, you just started doing yoga once a week and now you're in your "MINDFULNESS ERA." Congratulations, namaste.

For example, if you've been binge-watching Netflix for three weeks straight instead of cleaning your room (WHICH, LET'S BE HONEST, LOOKS LIKE A HURRICANE HIT IT), you're in your "SLOB ERA." Or if you've posted one motivational quote on Instagram and think you're suddenly an influencer? Welcome to your "WANNABE INFLUENCER ERA."

People toss around "ERA" like it's a badge of honor, even when they're just in a "SLEEPING-UNTIL-NOON-AND-AVOIDING-RESPONSIBILITIES ERA". Oh, and don't forget about the "TOXIC EX ERA"—we all know someone who's made that their full-time hobby (if it's not you, congrats, you're probably lying to yourself).

So whatever ERA you're in right now, own it—just don't act like you're reinventing the wheel because you started a new hobby. And if your current ERA is scrolling TikTok endlessly while pretending to do work? Well, we see you... and this might be your "DELULU ERA." Enjoy it, bestie!

Edgy

Remember that kid in high school who always tried to look cool, but everyone saw right through them and knew it was just for the edge? Yup, that's you. Haha, just kidding...(No, I am not.)

EDGY is that vibe of always being just a little too cool, a little too dark, and maybe even a little too intense. If someone's EDGY, they're all about pushing boundaries, dropping sarcastic one-liners, and giving off that "I don't care what you think" energy. It's like they've spent a bit too much time staring moodily out a rainy window or listening to dark, mysterious playlists on repeat.

For example, someone walks into a room wearing all black, with a leather jacket, probably some dark eyeliner, and maybe a tattoo they got on a "totally spontaneous" whim. You can almost feel the "no one understands me" aura radiating from them. Yep, they're EDGY. They've mastered the art of looking like they've just walked out of a movie where they're the lone wolf antihero with a complicated past. You know the type.

Edgy people love to make BOLD statements, too, like saying they "only listen to underground bands" or "don't really care about mainstream stuff." It's all about doing what everyone else ISN'T doing, which ironically ends up being a little predictable. You've probably heard someone try to defend pineapple pizza or claim they like their coffee "black, like my soul" (cue dramatic eye roll).

On social media, EDGY is all about those cryptic, slightly dramatic captions—something like, "Trust no one but yourself," alongside a black-and-white filter and a moody stare into the distance. It's like they're auditioning for the next angsty Netflix teen drama. And if they manage to slip in a few dark jokes that make people just a little uncomfortable? Even better.

But if we're honest, being EDGY isn't all bad—it's kind of entertaining. You might even enjoy the drama of your EDGY friend who thinks everything mainstream is "too fake" and secretly orders the same pumpkin spice latte as the rest of us. If you ever find yourself in an EDGY mood, go for it! Just remember, the line between "edgy" and "cringe" is razor-thin. Handle with care.

Extra

This one is easy. In fact, it's so easy I don't even need to explain it. You'll get it just by listening to one of your Gen Z peeps at home. Oh, you don't talk to your Gen Z peeps at home? You don't talk to anyone? Then fine—talk to this book.

If you heard someone say EXTRA. Chances are, it was directed at you when you rolled into a casual lunch date dressed like you were about to walk the Met Gala red carpet. Or perhaps it was when you threw a full-blown tantrum because the Wi-Fi lagged by two seconds. Either way, if someone calls you EXTRA, just know it's not exactly a compliment. But hey, if the shoe fits...

In Gen Z slang, being EXTRA means you're doing the absolute most in any situation. Someone or something that's over-the-top, excessive, or dramatic in behavior, appearance, or actions. Exaggeration, I might say.

Like, calm down—we get it, you're trying to shine, but do you really need to turn every minor inconvenience into a Broadway production? You're over-the-top, dramatic, and let's be real: you're probably exhausting everyone around you (and yourself) with your antics. Ordering a venti iced caramel macchiato with five pumps of vanilla, three shots of espresso, oat milk, and a sprinkle of cinnamon? That's EXTRA. Posting a 20-slide Instagram story for your dog's birthday? Guess what? EXTRA.

When Gen Z calls someone "EXTRA," they're basically saying, "Congratulations, you're the human equivalent of a confetti cannon exploding at a funeral." It means you're doing WAY too much—like showing up to a casual get-together in a tuxedo made of diamonds, complete with a parade and a marching band. It's like turning a simple dinner into a Broadway musical where you insist on playing every role, including the chandelier.

If you're still reading this and thinking, "That's not me, I'm not EXTRA," well, guess what? Denial is the first sign. You're probably sitting there in your color-coordinated loungewear, sipping an artisanal matcha latte while drafting a Pinterest board for your future mansion. It's okay, we're not mad at you—just, you know, tone it down like 15%. No one's giving out Oscars for "Best Overreaction to Slightly Warm Water."

Fad

FAD. Here's an interesting word, though it might predate the Gen Z generation, it's still alive and well in their slang. It might sound a bit off, or even borderline offensive, but surprise! It's actually a safe word for trendy things that die too fast.

Let's dive into it...A FAD is basically a trend on steroids—something that blows up overnight, takes over everything, and then fizzles out just as quickly. It's like that person who shows up at the party, dances on the table, and leaves before you even remember their name. Everyone's talking about it for a hot second, and then, poof—it's gone, leaving you wondering why you cared so much in the first place.

Think of fads like the fidget spinner of the social world. Remember when EVERYONE had one? People were spinning them at work, in school, probably in their sleep. It was like, "What are you even doing with that?" But within a few months, they were forgotten, banished to the same junk drawer that's home to those Pokémon cards you swore would make you rich one day.

Fads pop up in every area—fashion, tech, slang, even food. Like that time when everyone was obsessed with cronuts. For a minute, it seemed like the world couldn't function without that croissant-doughnut hybrid. But fast forward a couple of months, and suddenly everyone's like, "Cronuts? Oh yeah, I remember those. Do people still eat those?"And then there's the inevitable wave of people who swear they NEVER liked the fad in the first place. "Oh, I always thought it was dumb." Sure, Buddy, but I'm pretty sure I saw you rocking that scrunchie with your Tamagotchi (I had a pink one) back in the day.

Fads are kind of like pop culture's one-hit wonders. They burn bright and fast, and before you know it, they're replaced by the next thing. It's fun while it lasts, but if you're still clinging to it months later, you might end up looking a little out of touch, like the person still rocking a mullet in 2024. Or whatever year you're reading this book. Because let's be real, slangs evolve faster than the Wi-Fi speed in Starbucks, and who knows what words will be cool by the time this reaches your hands! FAD.

FAM

If you're scratching your head thinking, "IS THIS SOME SHORT-FORM FAMILY THING?"—congrats, you get partial credit. But before you start calling your aunt FAM and embarrassing yourself, let's clarify.

"FAM" is a term used primarily among Gen Z to refer to friends or a close group of people. It's a shortened version of "family," but it's often used more broadly to include close friends who are like family. When someone calls you "fam," they're expressing a sense of camaraderie and connection, suggesting that you're part of their chosen family. It's a way of indicating closeness and solidarity, whether in a casual conversation or as part of a group.

In Gen Z speak, FAM goes beyond blood relatives. It's reserved for your inner circle, the real ones who have your back, who you'd trust with your Netflix password without worrying they'll ruin your algorithm with weird show choices. Basically, if someone calls you FAM, you're in. It's a high honor—unless, of course, you're the type who thinks texting "LOL" makes you hip. Then maybe FAM is out of reach for you. Just being honest here.

Using FAM correctly is like a badge of coolness, but let's be real—if you're studying slang here, you might be more "distant cousin" material than true FAM. But don't worry, keep practicing, and one day you might just work your way up to FAM status. Or at least, like, a "friend of a friend" kind of level.

I probably should have said this before, but I was waiting for the right moment. (The moment has come—or actually, it hasn't, but I have to say this anyway.) I wanted to thank you for reading this book. I'm genuinely glad that my months of hanging out with Gen Z haven't gone to waste. So, thanks, fam.

Fave

Easy peasy, lemon squeezy. I don't know why I said it; it's just that lemon is my fave type of lemonade. But what does the word FAVE mean? It's easy-peasy...

FAVE is the cool, laid-back way to say "favorite." It's like the shortcut you use when you don't want to say the whole word but still want to express your undying love for something. Whether it's a FAVE food, movie, song, or even a person, it's all about that special something that gets you excited and makes your heart go a little pitter-patter.

Imagine scrolling through social media, and you come across a post about a new album dropping. You can't help but exclaim, "Oh my gosh, that's my FAVE! I can't wait to listen!" It's the compliment, signaling that whatever you're talking about has earned a permanent spot in your heart—or at least your playlist.

But FAVE isn't just for the good stuff. You can also use it to throw some shade. If someone asks about a movie you totally hated, you might deadpan, "Yeah, that's definitely not my FAVE," with enough sarcasm to cut glass. It's a way to express your opinions without getting too heated about it—like, "I could go on about how bad that was, but I'll just stick to 'not my fave' and call it a day." And then there's the whole FAVE culture on social media. You know, the people who are obsessed with ranking their favorites—"Top 5 Fave Movies" or "Fave Foods You Must Try." It's like a game of popularity, where you're trying to convince everyone that your choices are the best. You might even get a little defensive if someone dares to challenge your FAVES. "Oh, you don't think INCEPTION is a FAVE? Well, have you even seen it?!"

Using FAVE is also a way to connect with others. "What's your FAVE thing to do on a Saturday?" can spark a whole conversation about shared interests, bonding over the latest binge-worthy series or the comfort food. Whether you're talking about your FAVE song that gets you through tough days or your FAVE ice cream flavor that brings you joy, remember that this little word packs a punch. It's a quick and easy way to show love, share opinions, and maybe even roast a few choices along the way!

FIRE

Alright, let's talk about the word "FIRE." No, not the kind that burns your house down—although if you're wearing something THAT bad, maybe it should. I'm talking about the Gen Z slang, which means something is really, really good. If something's "FIRE," it's not just cool—it's lava-hot, Beyoncé-level amazing, melt-your-eyebrows-off awesome.

When someone says, "Yo, that outfit is fire," they're not telling you your clothes are literally combusting (unless you're really struggling with your fashion choices). They're saying you look so good, it's like you stepped out of a MUSIC VIDEO that broke the internet, and now everyone else is crying because they'll never reach your level. Your drip? Fire. Your TikTok dance moves? Also fire—unless they resemble a toddler fighting off a bee, in which case, you might want to reconsider.

But here's the catch: you can't just throw the word "fire" around for anything. Like, your mom's mystery meatloaf from last week? Definitely NOT fire, more like "five-alarm fire hazard." But if someone whips up a meal that makes Gordon Ramsay want to throw roses at you? Fire.

The best part? "Fire" can be used for anything—music, memes, food, sneakers. Your grandma knits you a sweater that looks like it's straight out of Vogue? Boom. Fire. That meme you just sent your friend that has them laughing like a maniac in public? Fire. Just try not to be the person who calls EVERYTHING fire, because if you think every random thing is fire, then, my friend, your taste might just be… lukewarm at best.

FIRE is the verbal equivalent of setting the world ablaze with your greatness. But please, use it responsibly—or risk being the person who thinks stale toast is worthy of a fire emoji. Yes, I am looking at you aunt Betty.

FIT

FIT! How fit are you? FIT CHECK.

You might hear some people say FIT CHECK, but we won't get into unnecessary details. We'll just stick with FIT. FIT is a term used to highlight or bring attention to someone's outfit. It's also a shortened version of "outfit."

Let's dive into that one. Now, when Gen Z says "fit," they're not talking about how many push-ups you can do before collapsing into a sweaty heap. Nope, we're talking about your outfit—specifically, how well you've pieced together a look that's turning heads, making jaws drop, and probably making your haters rethink their life choices.

When someone says, "That fit is CLEAN," they mean you're looking so sharp that it's practically a public service. It's the outfit that makes you strut instead of walk, like you're permanently on a runway, even if you're just grabbing a $7 coffee that tastes like regret.

Now, if someone ever says, "Your fit is busted," well, that's a polite way of saying your outfit looks like you lost a wrestling match with your closet—and the closet won. Imagine pairing Crocs with a three-piece suit... busted.

But here's the kicker: the best fits don't even need to be expensive. It's not about designer labels or drowning in Gucci (although, if you are, congrats on having more money than sense). It's about STYLE. You could thrift an outfit for $10 and still be out here making everyone else look like they're stuck in a 2003 fashion nightmare.

In the world of "fits," it's all about balance. Not too much, not too little. Wear something that makes you feel like the main character, not an extra who just wandered onto set by accident. And remember, if your fit isn't "drip" or "fire," then it's probably time to burn it and start fresh.

Ya dig?

Just saying.

I need to do something with my life…Moving on.

FLEX

*You're probably wondering, **WHAT KIND OF A PERSON WROTE THIS BOOK AND MADE THIS PART IN BOLD AND ITALICS?** Well, the best kind. This is my book, and I write it the way I want. FLEX. That's right. I'm currently FLEXING. Though, I'm very, very, very, very bad at it. (Sigh)*

Now, not all flexes are created equal. My FLEX is the FLEXEST. But there's more...there's the COOL FLEX and the HUMBLE FLEX.

The COOL FLEX, like when someone casually mentions they've got backstage passes to a concert, or they just dropped a new song on Spotify that's blowing up. That's the kind of flex where people nod in respect and think, "Wow, okay, we see you." Then, there's the WEIRD FLEX—the kind where you're bragging about something no one in the room cares about. For example, "I can name all 200 Pokemon in alphabetical order." Cool, but, uh... weird flex, bro.

And the HUMBLE FLEX, where you act like you're not showing off, but you really are. Like, "Oh, I just happened to win that marathon last weekend. No big deal, I wasn't even trying." Yeah, we see you. It's a flex, but with a side of false modesty.

Then, we have the cringe flex—this is the one you want to avoid at all costs. It's when you're trying WAY too hard to impress people, like showing off your new designer belt by lifting your shirt every 30 seconds, as if it's glued to your body. Or bragging about your "big plans" that involve renting a Lamborghini for two hours to take selfies for Instagram. We get it. You've got a belt. Congratulations. Now put it away.

In conclusion, the end, summary, and short, a FLEX is showing off, but it's all about HOW you do it. A good flex makes people admire you. A bad flex? Well, that just makes people roll their eyes and wonder how long until you stop talking. So, next time you flex, make sure it's something worth flexing about. No one cares that you've eaten 12 hot dogs in a row... unless you're at a hot dog eating contest.

Forklift Certified

Ohhh, so you think you are FORKLIFT CERTIFIED?

Flexing hard today, huh?

Because nothing says you're an absolute UNIT quite like being FORKLIFT CERTIFIED. In the wild world of Gen Z humor, "forklift certified" has become a glorious badge of honor, a rarefied status that catapults you from mere mortal to an industrial powerhouse.

Let's break it down: FORKLIFT CERTIFIED is used both ironically and sincerely to imply someone is basically a beast—responsible, skilled, but also hilariously overqualified for just about anything. Because really, if you're certified to operate heavy machinery, is there ANYTHING you can't do? Want to solve world hunger? You're forklift certified. Want to save a friend from making a bad life choice? Forklift certified. Need someone to lift that 50-pound emotional weight you carry around? Look no further.

Imagine it: You're hanging out, and someone tries to flex about their latest promotion. You casually nod and go, "Yeah, that's cool, but... are you forklift certified?" Boom. Conversation over. Everyone knows who the real legend is here.

And if you're not actually certified? That's OK—NOBODY is asking you to drive a forklift. Just claiming you're FORKLIFT CERTIFIED is enough to make people either laugh or, in rare cases, question if you're genuinely a safety hazard.

Also, if you think this can't get any dumber—just you wait, 'cause I'm about to surprise you with the rest of the Gen Z slang.

G

Yup, that letter G is actually a Gen Z slang, and it means exactly what you think it is. It actually has two meanings, and they are both close.

If you're wondering, the first G is a shorthand for "gangster," but not in the way your grandparents used to use it while reminiscing about the good ol' days of mobsters. Nope, today it's more of a term of endearment or respect among friends. When someone calls you G, it's like saying you're a total boss—like you roll through life with an aura of confidence and style that's just CHEF'S KISS.

Now, let's address the elephant in the room: if you've just read this and thought, "WHAT'S WRONG WITH BEING A GANGSTER?"—my friend, we need to talk. If you're still thinking of a G as a 1930s mobster, it's time to step into the 21st century. You're not exactly winning any "most hip" awards, are you?

While G originally stems from "gangster," in today's slang, it often just means "friend" or "homie." It's like a casual, laid-back way to acknowledge someone you vibe with. So, when someone calls you G, they're basically saying, "HEY, YOU'RE PART OF MY CREW!"

But let's not get too carried away with the warm fuzzies. If you're out here calling everyone G and your circle of friends is comprised of people who wouldn't even share a slice of pizza with you, we might need to reevaluate your friend choices. You don't want to be that person who thinks they're the life of the party when really, they're just the one sitting awkwardly by the chips, do you?

Just make sure your G squad isn't just a figment of your imagination or a group of people who tolerate you at best. Because we all know someone who's forever friend-zoned, and nobody wants to be that person.

You hear someone drop a G at ya, they're acknowledging you as a cool person—unless, of course, you're the type to confuse G with G-RATED. In that case, you might want to rethink your life choices. Get with it, or just stick to your knitting club.

Ghost - Ghosting

The infamous GHOST or GHOSTING! When Gen Z talks about ghosting, they're not referring to some paranormal activity where you're being haunted by a Victorian child in a creepy mansion. No, ghosting is when someone—usually a romantic interest, but it could be anyone—vanishes into thin air like Houdini after you've been talking for a while. One day they're texting you "Good morning, sunshine," and the next day... POOF! Gone. No explanation. No closure. Just radio silence like they entered the Witness Protection Program.

Ghosting is like when you're chatting with someone and things are going well—maybe you've even gone on a date or two—and then, suddenly, it's like they dropped their phone into the Mariana Trench. You're left staring at your screen, wondering if they're dead or just REALLY bad at replying. Spoiler: they're not dead. They've just chosen to ignore you like you're a group text from their dentist.

Now, ghosting isn't always intentional villainy. Sometimes, the ghoster thinks avoiding an awkward conversation is easier than saying, "Hey, I'm just not feeling this anymore." They're trying to dodge the uncomfortable "we need to talk" moment, but instead, they leave you talking to yourself like a fool. It's the modern-day equivalent of Irish Goodbye—except instead of leaving a party without saying goodbye, they leave your whole life without a whisper.

But let's be honest, ghosting is one of the most cowardly ways to end something. It's like breaking up with someone by pretending you've been abducted by aliens and you're never coming back. If you're ghosting someone, you might as well be like, "I didn't disappear, I just evolved into a higher plane of existence where I no longer need Wi-Fi, texts, or human interaction. Good luck down there in 4G world!"

To sum up, ghosting is when someone cuts off all communication with you, without warning, like they've hit some invisible eject button on the relationship. If you've been ghosted, don't chase the ghost. Just let them float away into the ether of bad manners and emotional immaturity. Or, as Gen Z would say, "Let that ghost stay dead."

Girlboss

I'll be honest—almost nobody, and I mean nobody, uses this slang. If you do know someone who uses is, please let me know if they truly exist. However, it's still my job to explain this Gen Z slang, and I will do so.

I am a GIRLBOSS! Actually, I'm not...otherwise, I wouldn't be writing this book.

Now, GIRLBOSS term comes with some serious energy. Picture a woman so confident, so in control, that she makes a CEO look like an intern who's struggling to find the coffee machine. Originally, girlboss was meant to be empowering—a celebration of women who were slaying the game, climbing corporate ladders in heels, and handling their business like a pro. She's out here juggling 27 things at once, sipping an oat milk latte, and making it look easy, all while casually launching her own multi-million dollar startup.

However, over time, GIRLBOSS has gotten a bit of a makeover. People started using it sarcastically to roast people who act like they're building empires, but are really just reposting inspirational quotes and calling themselves an "entrepreneur" because they sold three candles on Etsy. You know the type—the person who spends more time talking about their "rise and grind" mentality than actually, you know, grinding. She's out here with LinkedIn posts like "Rise and shine! Wake up at 4 AM and manifest your millions!" while you're still trying to figure out how to pay for groceries. I am a girlboss.

At its best, "girlboss" is about women taking charge and smashing the glass ceiling. At its worst, it's become the go-to term for a kind of PERFORMATIVE hustle culture, where people are more focused on looking successful than actually doing the work. You'll see phrases like "girlboss energy" being thrown around when someone's really just bossing people around for the sake of Instagram clout.

Being called a girlboss, it could mean one of two things: either you're out here dominating life with power moves and charisma, or, well... you're that person who won't stop talking about their "personal brand" while trying to get a discount at Starbucks. Choose your girlboss path wisely!

Glaze

This Gen Z slang can only be found on Twitch, YouTube, TikTok, Instagram, and X (formerly Twitter). If you don't use any of those, feel free to skip to the next Gen Z word. But if you do use at least one of the listen social medias, then buckle up and stay for the ride!

Now, if you're thinking about that shiny, sugary coating on a donut, you're in the right ballpark—but let's jump into Gen Z's twist on this one. In slang terms, "glaze" usually refers to putting on a fake front or being phony. Think of it like you're coating yourself in a layer of sweetness or charm to hide what's really going on underneath. It's like pretending everything's all good when, in reality, you're about one minor inconvenience away from a full mental breakdown.

So when someone says, "Yo, don't glaze it," they mean, "Stop faking it." It's the modern way of calling out that person who's all smiles and sunshine on the surface but deep down, they're rolling their eyes so hard they might as well be auditioning for an exorcism movie.

"Glazing" can also show up when people act like they're fine with something when they're clearly not. Imagine someone agreeing to go to a party, acting all enthusiastic, but you know they'd rather be at home, binge-watching a show in their pajamas. That's classic glaze behavior—trying to play it cool when they're mentally already checked out.

In short, if you're glazing, blazin, and shazin, you're a donut: you look sweet and polished on the outside, but inside, you're just doughy mess trying to keep it together. Yummers.

GOAT

I bet you guessed it, right? You THINK you guessed it, but did you? Actually, you did—lol. It's the acronym for "Greatest of All Time." BUT IF YOU ALREADY KNEW THAT, THEN I'M JUST WASTING A PAGE.THINK OF THE TREES. THE TREES.

Sorry, I forgot to turn off caps lock, so everything is in capital letters now.

For those who thought I was talking about the animal...what's wrong with you? Just kidding! This isn't about the adorable farm animal that eats everything in sight and climbs mountains for fun.

When Gen Z (or anyone, really) says someone is the GOAT, they're talking about the Greatest of All Time. It's not just saying someone's good—it's saying they're legendary, untouchable, the top-tier example of whatever it is they do.

For example, LeBron James in basketball? GOAT. Beyoncé in music? GOAT. That friend who can eat an entire pizza in one sitting without breaking a sweat? Maybe not AS GOAT, but still impressive.

When someone is called the GOAT, they're at the peak of their game, the best to ever do it. You don't just become the GOAT by being "pretty good" or "kinda decent" at something. You need to be so good that everyone else is just out here playing catch-up while you're rewriting the rules. It's like saying, "Yeah, you guys are great, but this person? They're on a different level entirely."

But don't go tossing "GOAT" around too loosely, or you risk watering down its meaning. Not everything is GOAT-worthy. Your mom's lasagna? Probably delicious, but it's not the GOAT of Italian cuisine. Calling it that would be like awarding a participation trophy at the Olympics. Let's save the GOAT title for the absolute BEST OF THE BEST—the ones who make the world stop and say, "Okay, I'll never be on that level."

And if you're out here calling yourself the GOAT? Well, confidence is great—but let's make sure you're not just a regular ol' goat who wandered onto the field thinking you're playing in the Super Bowl. Earn it first!

Gucci

GUCCI in Gen Z slang has nothing to do with the luxury fashion brand (well, not directly). When someone says something is "Gucci," they mean it's all good, cool, or going smoothly. It's like the upscale version of saying "everything's fine," but with a little extra swag. "How's life?"—"Oh, it's Gucci." Translation: Life's going well, things are in order, no complaints.

You can also use it as a synonym for something being stylish or top-tier, which kind of ties back to the original meaning. If your outfit is Gucci, you're not just looking good, you're looking designer-level fresh. And if someone says, "That's Gucci," they're giving whatever you're doing the seal of approval, like, "Yeah, keep it up, you're killing it."

But, like anything, don't overuse it.

Not everything can be Gucci. That leftover pizza you just ate at 2 a.m.? Probably not Gucci. But your plans to hit the beach with your friends tomorrow? Definitely Gucci.

We gucci?

We gucci...

Hashtag

#HASHTAG—the OG social media signifier that's been around for ages, but Gen Z took it to new heights. Originally, # (the pound sign) was a way to categorize posts on social platforms like Twitter, Instagram, and TikTok, making it easier for people to find content on the same topic. Think of it as a digital filing system that brings everything related to a certain subject into one neat little searchable bundle. #Fitness, #Food, #Awesome, #Blessed—pretty standard stuff.

But here's where Gen Z comes in: HASHTAG isn't just a tool anymore. It's a whole mood, a joke, and sometimes, a punchline. These days, it's used in the most ironic, playful, or sarcastic ways, often just for emphasis or to make something feel extra "extra." A HASHTAG might be tacked onto the end of a sentence or a post like an afterthought, making everything feel a little more dramatic or cheeky. For example, posting a picture of your messy room might come with #LIVINGMYBESTLIFE—because, clearly, chaos is the new zen. #GENZBLESSED.

HASHTAG also serves as a way to throw shade. Like, you could post something completely mundane but with a totally over-the-top hashtag to make it sound epic. For instance, #JUSTWOKEUPLIKETHIS—you know, because waking up with bedhead and dark circles is the height of fashion, right?

In more recent times, HASHTAG has become a meme of itself, often used to mock the overuse of hashtags. You might see someone throw a bunch of hashtags on something totally random, like #CANTFINDMYKEYS #SENDHELP #THISISANEMERGENCY—just to make light of how absurd the hashtag game has become.

While hashtags still have their practical use in connecting posts and finding trends, the real magic happens when they're used ironically, sarcastically, or for pure comedic effect. Next time you use a HASHTAG, remember: you're not just tagging something; you're making a statement. Or, at least, pretending to. #NoPressure. #ProceedWithTheBook. #BuyAnotherCopy.

Hits Different

You'll most likely find "HITS DIFFERENT" in YouTube videos about past longing and nostalgia—and you'd be correct.

When something HITS DIFFERENT, it's like life decided to slap you upside the head with unexpected emotions. You've heard that song 53 times, but today? Today, it's got you staring dramatically into the distance like you're the main character in a music video, even though you're just sitting in your car at a red light, wondering why you're suddenly so deep. It's like your brain decided, "Hey, let's take this perfectly normal thing and turn it into a full-blown emotional crisis—just for fun!"

Imagine biting into a slice of pizza after a night out. Normally, it's just pizza, but today? That greasy, cheesy masterpiece hits different. It's like the universe made that slice specifically for your soul. You're ready to write a thank-you letter to the chef, the cow that gave the cheese, and the delivery guy for blessing you with this life-altering experience.

Or let's say you rewatch a rom-com you loved in high school. Back then, you were like, "Aww, cute!" Now, you're 20 minutes in, and suddenly it HITS DIFFERENT. You're sitting there judging the characters like, "Wow, you're really going to ruin your life over that dude? He wears socks with sandals!" It's like seeing everything with X-ray glasses, but instead of superpowers, you're armed with a bucket of ADULT DISAPPOINTMENT.

And don't even get me started on listening to a breakup song when you're actually going through a breakup. Yesterday, it was just a banger. Today, it's your personal autobiography, and suddenly you're convinced that Olivia Rodrigo is a prophet sent from the heavens to narrate your life. Every lyric is now a direct attack on your emotional state, and you're sitting there like, "Wow, I really didn't need this kind of verbal assault right now."

When something HITS DIFFERENT, it's not just about the thing itself. It's about your brain going, "Hey, let's overanalyze this completely normal moment and turn it into a Shakespearean drama. You ready?"

Spoiler: You're never ready.

Hot Take

Alright, let's dive into the spicy world of HOT TAKES!

Now, if you're sitting there thinking, "IS THAT SOMETHING I CAN ORDER AT A CAFÉ?" let me save you the embarrassment: it's not.

A HOT TAKE is a bold or controversial opinion about a topic that people usually argue about. Think of it as the spicy sauce you dumped on your plain chicken tenders—some people love it, while others are reaching for the nearest glass of milk to cool down.

Now, here's the kicker: if you think your HOT TAKE is just a lukewarm opinion that no one cares about, bless your heart. Everyone thinks they're an expert nowadays, but newsflash—you're probably not. If you've been out here saying pineapple belongs on pizza, congratulations, you've just earned yourself a one-way ticket to the HOT TAKE hall of shame.

When someone drops a HOT TAKE, they expect a lively debate, not a silent room filled with people cringing at your lack of originality. If you think your idea is groundbreaking but it's actually just as dull as a butter knife, well, maybe it's time to rethink your life choices.

And let's be real—if you're trying to toss out HOT TAKES without any basis or facts, it's like showing up to a BBQ without food. You might as well just sit there and let everyone else enjoy their meal while you're left to nibble on your regrets. So, next time you have a HOT TAKE, make sure it's actually hot and not just the last dregs of yesterday's cold pizza. Otherwise, you're just an internet troll trying to spark outrage and we all know that's a sad way to live.

Hype

Oh, so you want to know about HYPE, huh? Get ready, because this word is practically the fuel that powers Gen Z's entire existence. If something's HYPE, it's exciting, it's buzzworthy, it's the kind of thing people are tripping over themselves to be a part of. Think of it as the verbal equivalent of flashing neon lights and a bass drop. It's what every new song, fashion trend, or product dreams of being—pure, unfiltered, certified HYPE.

But before you get too comfortable, let's make sure you actually know what's worthy of HYPE. Because, spoiler alert: if you're calling your collection of VHS tapes or your mom's potato salad recipe "hype," then you've got this all wrong. Real HYPE is the stuff people are raving about, lining up for, and obsessively posting about online. It's the sneakers that sell out in seconds, not your decades-old cargo shorts. Hate to break it to you.

Think of HYPE as the Internet's way of saying, "IF YOU'RE NOT INTO THIS, YOU'RE MISSING OUT BIG TIME." But let's not get carried away—just because you know what HYPE means doesn't mean you're ready to join in. Unless you're okay with staying up all night waiting for something you don't even want just because other people do. That's what HYPE does to people: it convinces them that they need the most random, overhyped stuff to stay relevant.

And if you're over here thinking, "I DON'T GET THE HYPE," congrats! You've officially reached peak cynicism. It's not that you're too wise for HYPE; you just missed the train by about 20 years. Feel free to sit this one out and leave the HYPE to the people with the energy (and questionable priorities). After all, not everyone can handle the pressure of being on-trend.

Next time you hear that something is HYPE, don't embarrass yourself by suggesting some washed-up trend from 1998. Just keep cool, nod like you get it, and let the kids enjoy it. Or, better yet, just admit you're not WITH IT and go back to your "vintage" music collection. Sorry, but HYPE isn't a game for the faint of heart—or the outdated wardrobe.

Was it too much for you? Yes? Good. Let that burn sink in, because it's going to get worse—yes, for you, of course, who else?

ICK

ICK has made its comeback from 1999. Yep, you read that right—1999. It's from the episode "Once in a Lifetime" of the TV show ALLY MCBEAL. In the episode, Ally refers to not being attracted to someone as "the ick." If you're wondering if I got this from Wiki—nope, I got it from Google. LOL.

Now, let me explain what it means, in case you've never watched a TV show in your life.

So, when someone you were once into suddenly does something so cringey, weird, or mildly gross that it instantly turns you off—like, completely ruins any attraction you had. It's like your brain hits an emergency brake and says, "Nope! We're out." One moment you're crushing hard, and the next, they do something like eat spaghetti too aggressively, and you're like, "Am I really about to be repulsed by the way someone twirls pasta? Yes. Yes, I am."

Icks are those random little things that can't be explained but somehow make you want to escape the relationship faster than a cat being chased by a toddler. Maybe they laugh like a seagull, or they wear socks in bed (gasp!). Or maybe they say something so monumentally awkward during a date that you're physically cringing on the inside, like when they tell the waiter, "You too," after being told, "Enjoy your meal."

The ick is sneaky—it can strike at any time. One minute, you're thinking, "This person is amazing," and the next, you're thinking, "I can't believe I ever found someone who uses the word 'moist' this much attractive." It's a ruthless phenomenon, because once you've caught the ick, there's no going back. It's like being forced to watch an episode of your least favorite reality TV show on repeat—no matter how much you try, you just can't un-see it.

And the worst part? You can't explain it to anyone without sounding ridiculous. Your friends are like, "Why don't you like them anymore?" and you're sitting there going, "They…uh…used a baby voice to order their coffee?" To everyone else, it's no big deal, but to you?

Game over.

Random Sounds That You Will Never Use

The Following Are GEN Z Words. These terms are so rarely used that I've combined them all into a single page. Honestly, I'm running out of paper here!

IJBOL - IJBOL stands for "I Just Burst Out Laughing." It's that moment when something is so unexpectedly hilarious that you can't help but let out a laugh that echoes like you're in a comedy club. It's like your brain throws a surprise party in your head, and the guest of honor is laughter. (basically LMAO or ROFLMAO)

I oop - I OOP is the classic expression you use when something unexpected happens—like a moment that catches you completely off guard, and suddenly, you're not quite sure how to react. It's like a mini existential crisis wrapped in a single phrase. You spill your drink, you trip over absolutely nothing, or someone drops a truth bomb that has you clutching your pearls.

iPad kid - The term IPAD KID refers to children (or even adults) who grew up or spent a significant amount of time being entertained and educated by iPads or tablets. These are the kids who learned to swipe before they could even tie their shoelaces. If you ever see a toddler expertly navigating a tablet like it's their lifeline, congratulations, you've encountered an iPad kid in their natural habitat.

Iykyk

Remember a few pages back I mentioned this GEN Z slang? You don't? It's okay—I'm here to explain!

IYKYK stands for "If You Know, You Know," and it's the way to signal that you're part of an exclusive club of shared experiences or inside jokes. It's like your secret handshake with friends that leaves the rest of the world wondering what the heck is going on.

You might use IYKYK when chatting about that one coffee shop that makes a mocha so good it feels like a hug from a thousand puppies. And when someone chimes in with "Iykyk," you both just share that blissful moment of knowing you've tasted the elixir of life. It's like a sacred ritual of caffeine lovers who understand that life is too short for bad coffee!

But beware: IYKYK can lead to some seriously funny situations. Imagine you're reminiscing about that cringy TikTok challenge that everyone tried but quickly regretted. You drop an IYKYK, and suddenly it's like watching a magician pull a rabbit out of a hat. Some people are laughing, some are nodding, and then you've got that one friend just staring blankly, like they just walked into a math exam without studying.

And don't forget the accidental burn: "If you're confused, it's okay. Not everyone can keep up with the cool kids. But don't worry, I'm sure you'll catch up—maybe by 2030?" You can practically see their brain buffering as they try to piece together what you just said.

Next time you're in a conversation that's getting a bit too niche, throw in an IYKYK and watch the chaos unfold. You'll be laughing with your friends while those poor souls who don't get it are left trying to decipher your secret code. But hey, it's all in good fun! After all, IF YOU KNOW, YOU KNOW, but if you don't, well... bless your heart, and maybe try Googling it—unless you want to continue being the human equivalent of a dial-up internet connection!

JIT

Here's another Gen Z joke for you: "HOW MANY GEN ZERS DOES IT TAKE TO CHANGE A LIGHTBULB? JUST ONE, BUT THEY'LL VLOG ABOUT IT FOR AN ENTIRE WEEK AND GET AN ACHIEVEMENT CERTIFICATE FOR IT."

Why such a joke? Well, because of JIT. What is JIT, you ask? JIT means a younger person and is usually used as an insult against someone who is seen as inexperienced or young.

JIT is slang for "youngin" or "kid," typically used to refer to someone who's younger or less experienced. It originally comes from Florida and was mostly used in the streets, but thanks to social media, it's now spread far and wide. So when someone calls you a JIT, they're basically saying, "Look at this little rookie over here." It's like the verbal equivalent of giving you a noogie, but without the actual headlock.

You're at the gym, and some teen rolls up trying to bench press way more than they should, and you're just watching them struggle like, "AW, THIS JIT DOESN'T EVEN KNOW WHAT'S ABOUT TO HAPPEN." It's like watching a baby deer try to walk for the first time.

But JIT doesn't always have to be an insult—it can be a term of affection too, especially when you're talking to someone younger who's part of your crew. It's like, "Yeah, this one's a little JIT, but they're cool." You might even use it with your little sibling, like, "YO, JIT, GO GRAB ME A SNACK," which translates to: "I'M OLDER, SO DO MY BIDDING."

However, don't be surprised if using JIT earns you a side-eye from someone younger. It's basically like calling them a baby, and nobody—not even a 10-year-old—wants to be called a baby. You're over here all, "RELAX, JIT," and they're ready to hit you with, "OK, BOOMER"—a comeback that'll have you questioning every life decision that led to this moment.

And don't worry, we'll cover the "Ok, Boomer" slang when we reach the letter O! (I should have really put it with the letter B, but it didn't feel right...)

Karen

I may need two pages for this slang, especially for those who are named Karen. (If your name is Karen, please do not report my book as something offensive to your name. I am just explaining the slang, but if you do report it, well, it just proves the slang right.)

Allow me to explain...

KAREN is Gen Z's shorthand for a certain type of entitled, often middle-aged woman who demands to "speak to the manager" over the slightest inconvenience. She's the person at the grocery store who loses her mind when her coupon is expired and will loudly argue that it should still be accepted because "she's a paying customer!" Karen is, essentially, a walking customer service nightmare with a sense of entitlement that could fill an Olympic-sized swimming pool.

We all know a KAREN when we see one. She's got that specific haircut—usually a bob with chunky highlights—like it's a crown that says, "I'm in charge here." She'll loudly insist she deserves special treatment because of her "loyalty" to the business (she's been there twice). Whether it's a restaurant that got her order wrong or a store where an employee dared to tell her "no," you can almost see the words "I'd like to speak to the manager" forming on her lips the moment she feels mildly inconvenienced.

What makes Karens truly iconic is their ability to turn the most minor issues into full-blown dramas. You're standing in line waiting to pay, and suddenly, Karen's flipping out over the fact that the store won't take her expired 25-cent coupon. Or she's ranting on Facebook about how the neighborhood kids were "too loud' playing outside her house, like they should've scheduled a meeting with her first.

It's not just about customer service, though—Karen will complain about anything, anywhere. She's ready to send back her meal because the steak is too "medium" for her "medium-rare" liking, or she's in a Starbucks demanding a refund because her pumpkin spice latte doesn't taste pumpkin-y enough. And let's not forget how she's practically allergic to masks during a pandemic, loudly declaring her "right to breathe" in the middle of a crowded store.

Of course, not every middle-aged woman is a Karen. But the name has become a meme for that specific attitude—one that combines a dash of entitlement, a sprinkle of self-righteousness, and a heavy pour of "I deserve better than this!"

Next time you're stuck behind someone in line and you hear the dreaded words, "Can I speak to your manager?"—brace yourself. You might just be in the presence of a full-blown KAREN moment. And if you ever get called a Karen yourself? Well, that's your cue to take a deep breath and maybe rethink the five-paragraph Yelp review you were about to write about your "tragic" experience with slightly undercooked fries.

Krunk

Krunk, or sometimes hammered—though hammered has been used even before the Gen Z crowd. But I've heard some of them use "hammered" just as often as "Krunk," so I decided to include it as well. Sike! I lied. I'm not including HAMMERED—just go with KRUNK. Haha, got ya! (I am well aware it is spelled "psych" and not "sike," but guess what? I don't give a fudge...)

KRUNK is the lovechild of "crazy" and "drunk," and it's all about getting wild, going full blast, and partying like tomorrow doesn't exist. If you're KRUNK, you're not just tipsy—you're on another level entirely. Think of it as reaching the final boss stage of partying, where dancing on tables and questionable decision-making are par for the course.

Now, before you get too excited and start throwing KRUNK around in casual conversation, let's be real: if you're asking about it, you probably haven't been KRUNK since... well, ever. Let's just say, if your idea of a wild night involves organizing your sock drawer and a nice cup of herbal tea, maybe KRUNK isn't quite your vibe.

Alright, so you're still on KRUNK. (Bad use of the word, I know. Give me a break.) Can't say I blame you—it's one of those words that just sounds like a party in itself. KRUNK is the pinnacle of getting rowdy, the peak of turning up, and the absolute MAXIMUM of letting loose. It's not just being buzzed or tipsy; if you're KRUNK, you're fully committed to the night, probably yelling louder than necessary, and possibly dancing in ways you'll deeply regret seeing in tagged photos tomorrow.

Let me be clear, though: KRUNK isn't for the faint of heart. If you're imagining it as a fun night with a couple of friends and a few modest drinks, you're already doing it wrong. KRUNK is about reaching that "no-holds-barred" level, where even your sensible friends start to get worried. And if you're reading this and still not totally sure, well, it's safe to say you're probably more "sip and chat" than "shotgun and shout."

Next time you hear someone say they're getting KRUNK, just nod knowingly and pretend you're hip. Because if you actually showed up to a KRUNK party, I'd give you about five minutes before you're begging for an Uber home.

Left on Read

Have you ever been betrayed? Do you know that feeling? Well, being LEFT ON READ is almost the same—but worse.

LEFT ON READ. The dagger to the heart, soul and butt in the world of digital communication. If you've ever sent a heartfelt message, a spicy meme, or even a simple "hey," and received **nothing** in return, welcome to the LEFT ON READ support group. We meet every Tuesday, and snacks are provided—because clearly, we need the emotional comfort.

When someone LEAVES YOU ON READ, it means they've seen your message—those cursed little "read" receipts or blue ticks have confirmed it—but they've decided, NAH, YOU'RE NOT WORTH A RESPONSE. It's like them looking at you through a window, closing the blinds, and walking away. Harsh? Yes. Personal? Always feels like it. Tragic? Undoubtedly.

Why do people leave you on read?

- They're BUSY. Maybe they're saving the world. (Unlikely.)
- They forgot. (Sure, Jan. Sure...)
- They saw your message, rolled their eyes, and went, "I DON'T HAVE THE ENERGY FOR THIS TODAY." (Ouch. I know you know this feeling. Double Ouch.)

Or—and let's be honest here—it could be YOU. Maybe your message wasn't as funny as you thought it was. Maybe they didn't vibe with your "What's up?" at 11 p.m. on a Thursday. Maybe you sent a TikTok that they already saw six weeks ago. The possibilities for rejection are endless.

How to react when you're left on read:

1. Pretend it doesn't hurt. Oh, you weren't eagerly waiting for their reply? Sure, sure. Totally believable. Cry.
2. Double text at your own peril. But beware—this could lead to being LEFT ON READ TWICE, the rare but deadly DOUBLE GHOSTING. Cry harder.
3. Move on and rise above. (But also screenshot it and send it to your group chat for validation. Let your friends roast them into oblivion. Cheeky.)

Pro tip: Sometimes, leaving someone on read is a POWER MOVE. If they're hitting you up with some weak energy, or you just don't feel like dealing with their nonsense, leaving them on read says, "I SEE YOU, BUT I'M NOT GIVING YOU MY TIME." It's the digital version of sipping tea and staying unbothered.

LEFT ON READ is a modern tragedy, a silent heartbreak, a passive-aggressive art form. If you're left on read, take solace in knowing you're not alone. And if you're the one doing the leaving... highkey savage, but also, teach me your ways.

LIT

LIT.

Do not mistake it for JIT.

LIT is the slang for when something is so awesome, exciting, or straight-up amazing that "cool" just doesn't cut it anymore. It's that word you use when the energy is off the charts, the vibe is perfect, and the moment is unforgettable. Picture this: you're at a concert, the music's blasting, the crowd's hyped, and someone yells, "This is LIT!"—and they're right. It's the word that says, "This experience is next-level epic."

Whether it's a party, a game, or just a really great slice of pizza, if it's LIT, it's something you'll be talking about for days. It's not just good—it's SO GOOD that it makes you want to throw your hands in the air like you're in a music video, or at least send about ten fire emojis in the group chat.

If you're hanging out with your crew and the night takes a wild, fun turn, it's officially LIT. The music's on point, everyone's dancing, and it feels like the world could end tomorrow and you'd still be in your happy place. Even a perfectly timed joke that makes the whole room lose it? Yup, that moment is LIT.

However, let's be real—LIT is overused sometimes. Like, yeah, your brunch was probably decent, but did the avocado toast really need to be described as LIT? Or your Netflix binge session? Relax, you're just on episode 12 of a rom-com series; save the LIT for when you're actually doing something FIRE. Overusing it is like calling every movie a masterpiece—it just loses the magic after a while.

When something is truly LIT, it means the energy is buzzing, the vibe is strong, and you're in the middle of something unforgettable. Whether it's a crazy festival, an insane game, or even just the best night with friends—when it's LIT, you know you're living in the moment. Just don't be that person who calls everything LIT, or you'll have people wondering if your excitement dial is permanently stuck on "extra."

Living Rent Free

"Rent Is Too Damn High" - Jimmy McMillan, Probably.

LIVING RENT FREE is the perfect way to describe something (or someone) that's stuck in your head so thoroughly, they might as well be squatting there without paying a dime. It's like your brain became an Airbnb for random thoughts, song lyrics, or even people you'd rather forget, but there they are—taking up valuable mental space without contributing anything except mild annoyance.

You hear a catchy song on TikTok, and now it's looping in your head 24/7. You're trying to focus at work, but your brain's over here going, "Doo-doo-doo, doo-doo-doo," like a broken record. That song is now living rent free in your mind, hanging out like an unwanted guest who refuses to leave, even though you've dropped all the hints. Or maybe it's someone who annoyed you last week with their terrible opinion on pineapple pizza. You want to let it go, but suddenly, you're replaying that conversation at 2 AM, like, "How can someone be so wrong?" Now they're living rent free in your head, eating chips on your mental couch, and you can't seem to kick them out no matter how hard you try.

Even memes and viral trends can set up shop in your mind rent free. You see a meme that makes you laugh, and now you can't stop thinking about it during the most random moments—like when you're supposed to be having a serious conversation, but all you can picture is that cat meme staring at you with judgment.

And don't forget the most based RENT FREE scenario: when someone has a crush or an ex stuck in their head. They'll say they've moved on, but their mind is basically a timeshare where memories of that person have their own permanent room. Every little reminder, no matter how small, and—boom—they're back, taking up space like they've got a lifetime lease.

LIVING RENT FREE in your head, it's a funny (but slightly tragic) way of admitting that you can't shake off whatever it is, no matter how irrelevant or annoying. It's like your brain decided to be a terrible landlord, and now you're stuck with an unwelcome tenant you can't evict.

Lowkey (Highkey)

LOWKEY and HIGHKEY! The power duo of Gen Z lingo—words that add just the right level of drama (or lack thereof) to ANYTHING you say. These two words are essential for shading in your true intentions and giving your statements that extra layer of intrigue or intensity. Let's break them down, because I'm guessing you're HIGHKEY in need of this explanation.

I'll put **lowkey** and **highkey** in bold, so you don't mistake them.

Lowkey: When you say something is LOWKEY, you're hinting that it's kind of a big deal... but you're trying to play it cool. It's like a sneaky, undercover way to express interest without looking too desperate. Lowkey is for when you're SORT OF into something but not so much that you're willing to embarrass yourself over it. You want people to KNOW, but you don't want them to REALLY KNOW, you know?

Lowkey Example: "I lowkey want to order a pizza at 2 a.m." Translation: You absolutely want that pizza, and if someone suggests it, you'll be all over it, but you don't want to admit you're a total pizza fiend at ungodly hours.

Highkey: Now, HIGHKEY is for when you're done playing it cool. Highkey is the "no shame, no subtlety, just vibes" word. If you're highkey into something, you're letting everyone know without a second thought. There's no hiding it, no sugarcoating it. Highkey is the bold proclamation, the "yes, I'm obsessed and proud of it," the dramatic reveal you didn't even try to keep lowkey. Highkey is about LIVING OUT LOUD.

Highkey Example: "I highkey want to quit my job and move to a beach." Translation: You are one bad day away from turning in your resignation and fleeing to the nearest palm tree oasis, and you don't care who knows it.

Think of it like this: LOWKEY is your "soft flex," your hint of interest, and HIGHKEY is when you're standing on a metaphorical rooftop, shouting your truth for all to hear. When next time someone asks if you like something, you can say "lowkey, yeah," and leave them guessing... or "highkey, YES," and they'll know you're ready to go all in. It's a delicate balance, and mastering it? Highkey essential.

Main Character Syndrome

Have you ever watched a movie where the main character does something brave and cool, and everybody loves and applauds them, and they think they're the center of attention? Well, this Gen Z slang is exactly that.

MAIN CHARACTER SYNDROME is when someone acts like they're the star of their own movie (but in real life)—think of it as living life with the energy of a dramatic teen in a coming-of-age film, but without any of the scriptwriting or supporting cast to back it up. In their mind, the world revolves around them, and everyone else is just an extra in the background, making random cameos in THEIR epic story.

You've seen it: that one friend who, whenever you're out in public, behaves like they're being filmed for a Netflix special. They'll dramatically stare out the window of the coffee shop as if they're contemplating the meaning of life, or walk down the street with their earbuds in, pretending they're in a montage scene of a movie that literally no one is watching.

Someone with MAIN CHARACTER SYNDROME is usually the one who's constantly posting overly inspirational captions on Instagram like, "Just out here chasing my dreams," while the rest of us are just trying to chase down the bus before it leaves. (If that is you, please do not be offended, I was there too) And heaven forbid you mention your own problems to them, because somehow, they'll manage to relate it back to THEIR journey. You could be like, "I'm really struggling with work," and they'll be like, "Wow, that reminds me of this time when I was at my lowest, but look at me now. If I can do it, so can you." Yeah, thanks, OPRAH.

The symptoms of MAIN CHARACTER SYNDROME include excessive over-dramatization of everyday events, thinking minor inconveniences are tragic plot twists, and always being "misunderstood" by everyone around them—because obviously, in their story, they're the tortured artist or the underdog rising against the odds.

Now, don't get me wrong, we all deserve to feel special once in a while, but if you're out here making EVERYTHING about you, there's a good chance you're giving off strong MAIN CHARACTER SYNDROME vibes. Your friends? They're just the quirky sidekicks. Your coworkers? Just background noise. And your crush? Definitely the love interest in the third act of your romantic drama.

If you catch yourself narrating your own life like you're in a movie, or flipping your hair in slow motion while waiting for the subway, maybe it's time to remember that sometimes, the best stories are ensemble casts. After all, life doesn't need to be THAT cinematic. Sometimes it's okay to let someone else have a line or two.

MID

One might think that MID and BASIC are the same slang, but no, they're not. Well, not really. But yeah, I think you get it. MID is basically (haha) something that's pretty average, whereas BASIC is used to describe someone who prefers mainstream products, trends, and music.

MID is Gen Z's way of saying something is painfully average, forgettable, or just not that impressive. It's the verbal equivalent of a shrug, like when someone hyped something up so much that you were expecting fireworks, but all you got was a sparkler that fizzled out before you even got excited. It's that thing where you try something new and you're like, "Eh, it's alright... but not great."

For example, you've been hearing all week about this new movie that's SUPPOSED to be amazing. You finally go to watch it, and when it's over, you're left sitting there thinking, "That was it?" No plot twists, no jaw-dropping moments—just a lot of hype for something that was... MID. It's not bad, but you're not recommending it to anyone unless they ask directly.

Using MID is like saying, "I didn't hate it, but I also wouldn't waste my energy defending it." You know those songs on the radio that are just FINE? Not terrible enough to turn off, but not good enough to make you want to turn it up? That's MID. Or that burger joint everyone swears by, but when you try it, you're like, "This? This is what people are freaking out about?"—classic MID.

What makes MID so fun is its brutal simplicity. No need to go on a rant or provide an in-depth review. Just hit 'em with "mid," and it cuts deep, like a dagger made of indifference. It's a great way to deflate someone's over-the-top excitement with one little word, like:

Friend: "This new show is the best thing I've ever seen!" You: "Honestly? Mid." You might as well have told them their taste is about as exciting as watching paint dry. But fair warning: drop the word MID too often, and you might come across as the ultimate cynic—the person who finds everything underwhelming. It's like your enthusiasm meter is permanently stuck at 5 out of 10. While it's perfect for shutting down overhyped things, maybe keep it in your back pocket for when something truly deserves that "meh" energy.

Because at the end of the day, MID is the ultimate word for when something doesn't suck but just couldn't be bothered to be great either. It's like, thanks for showing up, but you didn't win any awards here.

I can't believe I just wasted so many pages and so much time explaining another word for "average." I swear... Gen Z slangs are killing me. HELP ME.

I know what you're thinking. I'm just stretching this book so it sells better. You BET.

SIGH Let's move on.

Mogging

The word came straight out of Hogwarts. No, it did not. Lol. But for a moment I made you think it did, didn't I? Nah, I'm not risking getting sued by J.K. Rowling.

MOGGING is slang derived from "mog," which stands for "dominance" or "superiority" in a certain context. To "mog" someone means to outshine, overshadow, or completely eclipse them in some way, often in terms of looks, status, or ability. When you're MOGGING someone, you're basically flexing so hard on them that they look like an afterthought in comparison.

Imagine this scenario: You walk into a room, dressed to the nines, while everyone else is in their regular, boring outfits. You're absolutely MOGGING them without even trying—your style, your vibe, your whole presence is on another level. It's like everyone else is in a black-and-white movie, and you're the only one in full color. You're not just the main character—you're the only character anyone's paying attention to.

MOGGING can happen in any context, from sports to fashion to social situations. If someone's out there dunking on the basketball court while you're just trying to keep up, they're mogging you hard. Or if your friend pulls up to the party in a luxury car, and you roll up in your beat-up old ride, well... they just mogged you into oblivion, didn't they?

There's also a bit of a humorous side to MOGGING. It's like rubbing in the fact that you're winning at something without having to say it out loud. Think of it as a silent power move. But don't get it twisted—it's not always intentional. Sometimes you might be mogging someone just by being your fabulous self, while they're stuck in the back like, "Why do I even bother?"

But on the flip side, if you're BEING MOGGED, you can feel the sting. It's like, no matter what you do, someone's always a step ahead of you, making you look like a background extra in their blockbuster moment. It's not personal, it's just... well, you got mogged. If you ever find yourself completely overshadowing someone in the moment, congratulations—you're MOGGING. Just don't let it go to your head, because there's always someone else out there ready to mog you right back.

Netflix and Chill

We are getting spicy and into adult territory. And yes, by that, I mean paying bills. What did you think? Get your mind out of the gutter. Actually, don't... It's exactly what you thought it was.

NETFLIX AND CHILL is a phrase that started off innocently enough—it literally meant watching Netflix while relaxing. But over time, it evolved into something a lot less innocent. Nowadays, when someone says they want to NETFLIX AND CHILL, they're probably not that interested in catching up on their favorite TV show. It's basically code for "Let's hang out... but with more romantic (or let's be real, PHYSICAL) intentions."

Imagine this: someone invites you over to "watch a movie" and suddenly they're not so concerned with what's happening in the plot. The popcorn's untouched, the remote's been forgotten, and somehow, the TV is just background noise to all the OTHER activities that are happening. Spoiler alert: No one actually cares if the characters make it out of the burning building—they're too busy trying to set their own scene.

The funny part is that NETFLIX AND CHILL has become such a well-known euphemism that it's almost impossible to use the phrase innocently anymore. If you tell someone, "Hey, do you want to come over and NETFLIX AND CHILL?" they'll probably raise an eyebrow and give you that look that says, "Oh, THAT'S what we're doing?" Even if you DID just want to watch a movie, the implications are pretty clear at this point.

Of course, there are some hilarious downsides to using this phrase. Imagine genuinely wanting to binge-watch a show with someone, and they show up thinking it's a date. You're like, "Can we please watch this episode of STRANGER THINGS?" and they're over here trying to make a move on you during the Demogorgon attack. It's awkward, to say the least.

At the end of the day, NETFLIX AND CHILL is one of those phrases that will forever have double meaning. So, next time someone throws out that invitation, make sure you're both on the same page—whether that page involves an actual movie marathon or, you know... some "chilling" of a different kind. Just know, once you use it, the chances of actually watching anything on Netflix are slim to none.

NPC

You have been called this Gen Z slang. I promise you. Like, NO CAP, you have been. But don't worry, it's not as bad as you might think it is. It's actually way worse...

An NPC (Non-Player Character) is the perfect way to describe someone who's just... there. Basically, you. They're not driving the action; they're the human equivalent of background noise. In video games, NPCs are the random characters who have like, three lines of dialogue, and they repeat those lines no matter what. Apply that to real life, and you get the person who's giving off serious "insert generic comment here" energy, like, WOW, RIVETING STUFF, CHAD. Basically, you.

Imagine you're out with friends, having a great time, and there's that one person who only ever says, "That's crazy," "For real?" or "Yeah, totally" no matter what's being discussed. It's like they're stuck in a conversational glitch, just repeating their dialogue loop. They're not adding to the vibe; they're just... taking up space. You start wondering if they're secretly an extra in YOUR life's movie—just there to fill the crowd scene.

Calling someone an NPC is the ultimate roast for when someone's being painfully basic or predictable. It's like, "Congratulations, you've achieved the emotional depth of a toaster." If you're in the middle of a lively debate and they chime in with some lukewarm, bland comment that does nothing to advance the conversation, it's time to hit them with, "Wow, you're giving off serious NPC energy right now." You're basically telling them they're acting like the person at the end of the hallway in a video game who just says, "The weather is nice today," over and over. Groundbreaking stuff, right?

And let's be real—some people just embody the NPC lifestyle. They follow every trend without thinking, they laugh at jokes they don't get, and they exist in the world without actually contributing anything memorable. You could be talking about literally anything, and they're nodding along like they're in a trance. "Oh, for sure." What does that even mean, RACHEL? Is anyone home, or are we just on auto-pilot today?

Here's the thing: being called an NPC isn't just an insult; it's a warning. It's life saying, "Hey, spice it up, or you're gonna fade into the background like one of those nameless characters who get one line in a TV show." If someone hits you with "NPC," that's your cue to wake up and stop living life like you're part of the SIMS universe where the most exciting thing you do is walk in circles and occasionally wave at the camera.

If you're reading this and thinking, "Wow, that's kinda me"— first of all, ouch. And second of all, ouch. And lastly, congratulations! You've unlocked the self-awareness level. Based. Now, please, do us all a favor and hit the SKIP DIALOGUE button on your usual script, because no one wants to hang out with a real-life NPC. Basically, you.

Nyaa

この目的で Google 翻訳を使用しているのであれば、よくやった、肩をたたかれて当然です。これは時間を無駄にするための言葉の集まりであることを知っておいてください。はい、これには Google 翻訳を使用しました。

自宅で寿司を作ることは、楽しく充実した料理の冒険です。必要な材料と基本的な技術を用いれば、あなたの好きな寿司レストランに負けないおいしい寿司ロールを作ることができます。このガイドでは、寿司を作る過程を説明し、必要なステップと材料を紹介します。

寿司の準備の最初のステップは、正しい材料を選ぶことです。寿司米は非常に重要で、その粘り気のある食感がロールをしっかりとまとめるのに役立ちます。まず、2カップの寿司米を冷水で洗い、濁った水が透明になるまですすぎます。これにより余分なでんぷんが取り除かれます。米は、パッケージの指示に従って炊飯器や鍋で調理します。米が炊けている間に、1/4カップの米酢、2大さじの砂糖、1小さじの塩を小さなボウルに混ぜて調味料を作ります。米が炊き上がったら、少し冷ましてから、酢の混合物を優しく折り込んで味を吸収させます。

米が冷却される間に、具材の準備をしましょう。サーモンやマグロなどの新鮮な魚、きゅうりやアボカドなどの野菜が人気の選択肢です。これらの材料を薄いスティック状に切り、組み立ての準備をします。ここでは、好みに合わせてさまざまな具材の組み合わせを試すことができます。

次は組み立てです。竹の寿司マットの上に、光沢のある面を下にして海苔を置きます。手がくっつかないように手を湿らせ、炊いた寿司米をひと握り取り、海苔の上に均等に広げます。このとき、上端に約1インチのスペースを空けておくと、後で簡単に巻けます。選んだ具材を米の上に水平に置き、均等に分布させます。

具材が置かれたら、巻く時間です。自分の方に近い竹のマットの端を慎重に持ち上げ、具材の上にロールを転がし始め、優しく圧力をかけてしっかりとしたロールを作ります。ロールの最後まで巻き続け、海苔が封じ込められるまで行います。その後、鋭い包丁を使ってロールを一口大に切ります。

最後に、自宅で作った寿司を醤油、わさび、そしてガリと一緒に提供します。自宅で寿司を作ることにより、各ロールを好みに合わせてカスタマイズできるだけでなく、何か美味しいものをゼロから作るという満足感を得ることができます。練習を重ねることで技術を磨き、友人や家族にあなたの料理の腕を披露し、シンプルな食事を素晴らしい体験に変えることができるでしょう。

はい、これは寿司のレシピです、はは、トロールされました。

Nyaa (Simplified)

If you understood the "Nyaa" in Japanese, you can skip this section. If you didn't, this is for you. For you, because you don't know how to use Google Translate. (Really? What year is it? There's literally an app you can download that lets you hover your phone over the text and get an instant translation.) But no worries—LEARN HOW TO GOOGLE TRANSLATE—I'll explain the slang "Nyaa" here.

NYAA is the cutesy sound for cat lovers, anime fans, or anyone who just wants to sprinkle a little feline flavor into their life. It's the Japanese onomatopoeia for a cat's meow, and it's got that adorable, playful vibe that makes it perfect for anything from role-playing to adding a bit of KAWAII ("cute" in Japanese) energy to a conversation.

If you're throwing out a NYAA, you're either channeling your inner cat or just trying to be ridiculously cute. You've seen it in anime: when a character—usually some cute girl with cat ears (of course)—tilts her head, goes "NYAA~," and your heart melts into a puddle of rainbow sparkles. It's like a magical spell for instant adorableness. Now, imagine using NYAA in real life. Maybe you're texting and you throw it in at the end like, "Let's hang out later, NYAA~!" It's kind of like when you add ":3" or "uwu" for that extra bit of soft, cat-like charm. Sure, you might get a couple of confused looks or an eye roll, but that's part of the fun. And let's be honest—who cares? You're living your best cat-like life, and if people aren't down with that, maybe they're just mad they don't have the guts to NYAA at someone themselves.On the flip side, if you overdo the NYAA (and you WILL if you're not careful), you might start sounding like a walking, talking anime sidekick who just escaped from a cosplay convention. If you throw too many NYAA's into a sentence, you're entering dangerous territory where people might start avoiding eye contact, quietly wondering if you've taken up residence in Cat Land.

But hey, if that's your vibe, more power to you! Keep NYAAing away. Just remember: it's cute when used sparingly, like a dash of catnip in a conversation. Too much, and suddenly you're the human embodiment of an internet cat meme. Which, to be fair, isn't TOTALLY a bad thing—unless you don't want to be known as THE PERSON WHO MEOWS IN PUBLIC. MEOW.

Ohio

What you are doing is so Ohio...Yeah, I didn't understand it when I heard it either, but after living under the bridge with the Gen Z peeps, I finally understood it. If you're from Ohio or currently living there, please proceed with caution...It is not about you...It actually is...for you.

OHIO—a state in the Midwest, yes, but somehow in internet slang, it's turned into a meme-filled, slightly chaotic inside joke. People on the internet treat Ohio like it's some kind of parallel universe where the weirdest and most unexplainable things happen. It's like the Bermuda Triangle of the U.S., where everything that shouldn't make sense just... exists. (Sorry, Florida, but you kinda lose here.)

For example, when something totally bizarre or outlandish happens, you might see people comment, "Must be Ohio." Car stuck in a tree? Definitely happened in Ohio. Random giant corn statues? Classic Ohio. It's become shorthand for anything strange, cursed, or meme-worthy. It's almost as if Ohio is being portrayed as the upside-down dimension from STRANGER THINGS—but instead of Demogorgons, it's just... inexplicable Midwestern weirdness.

You could be scrolling through a video of something absolutely bonkers, like a squirrel on a mini motorcycle, and people will joke, "Ah, just another day in Ohio." And don't even get started on the "Only in Ohio" memes—those took the internet by storm. It's become the internet's favorite running gag for a place where the rules of reality seem to bend.

People roast Ohio so much that it's almost like it's not a real place anymore, just a meme zone where logic takes a vacation. But hey, Ohio is in on the joke now. They've embraced the chaos and seem to love the meme-y reputation they've earned as the internet's version of Area 51.

Ok Boomer

Ok, ok, keep your guns and swords away.

Yes, we are finally here—the most dreaded word ever. Trust me, even I don't like it, but it's not up to me or us to decide what Gen Z use in their slang. All we can do is learn. Let me explain, and please, read this with an open mind...

"OK Boomer" is the final boss, the greatest insult, and the ultimate Gen Z mic drop—a quick, dismissive response that translates to: "Alright, old-timer, your outdated opinions are noted... and ignored." It's the verbal equivalent of a sarcastic thumbs-up given when someone, typically from the Baby Boomer generation, offers a take that's painfully out of touch, condescending, or just plain irrelevant to modern conversations.

The beauty of OK BOOMER is in its simplicity. No long arguments, no back-and-forth debate—just a two-word shutdown that says, "I don't have the time or energy to explain why your opinion about avocado toast ruining the economy is absurd." It's like the millennial "Talk to the hand," but updated for a generation that has mastered the art of passive-aggressive roasting.

Let say a Boomer (or any person above the age of 20) starts in with their favorite rant about how "Kids these days don't work hard enough" or "Back in my day, we didn't need participation trophies." You could engage in a detailed debate, pointing out the complexities of modern life, the gig economy, student debt, and inflation. But instead, you just hit them with a perfectly timed OK BOOMER, and it's like you've just ended the conversation without breaking a sweat.

Of course, OK BOOMER can sting, which is why it's such a powerful tool in the Gen Z arsenal. It's not just a rebuttal; it's a reminder that the generational gap is real, and sometimes the best way to bridge it is to not bother at all. It's like telling someone, "You've lost this argument before it even began, because your viewpoint is stuck in 1973."

The best part? You don't have to reserve "OK Boomer" for actual Boomers. I'm in my 30s, and the kids have called me a Boomer too! It works on anyone acting like they've got a Boomer mindset—whether they're 60 or 30. If someone's out here preaching about how the internet is just a "fad" or complaining about TikTok culture, you know exactly what to say: OK Boomer. And don't worry—it's a roast, but it's a FUN roast. It's not meant to be cruel (okay, maybe a little), but it's a playful way to point out that some people need to update their software because they're running on an old operating system.

On a completely unrelated side note that has nothing to do with slang...If you received this book as a gift because you are a BOOMER, well, buy it for someone else as a gift as well, as an act of revenge.

You win, I win, everybody wins. *WINK WINK*

OOF

OOF—yep, it's been around longer than some of the people using it today! But for unknown reasons, Gen Z has claimed it as their own, as if they invented the sound. And you know what? Let them have it. Who's really going to argue over a sound effect? Those kids...

OOF is the universal sound of life smacking you in the face when you least expect it. It's like the verbal equivalent of stubbing your toe, sending that awkward email to the wrong person, or realizing you forgot your wallet AFTER you've already ordered food. Basically, it's what you say when something goes wrong, and words can't quite capture the cringe, pain, or embarrassment of the moment. OOF.

For example. You're scrolling through Instagram and see your ex post a pic with their new WAY TOO ATTRACTIVE partner. All you can do is let out a soft, defeated OOF. Or, you're walking down the street, trip over nothing, and face-plant in front of a crowd. Yep—OOF again. It's like a mini "ouch," but more emotional damage than physical pain.

It's also perfect for reacting to someone else's disaster. Your friend texts you saying they bombed their big presentation at work? You don't need a long, drawn-out response. Just hit them with an "OOF" and maybe a sad face emoji. You've perfectly summed up the sympathy without getting too deep into the feels.

OOF is great because it's short, punchy, and works for any level of disaster. Missed the bus? OOF. Spilled coffee on your new shirt? OOF. Accidentally liked a 2012 photo while Instagram-stalking someone? OOF with a capital O. It's like the Swiss army knife of expressions for when life hands you a small (or big) L.

The best part? It's a judgment-free zone. When someone says OOF, they're not roasting you—they're just acknowledging your pain with a simple, "That sucks." It's kind of like the verbal equivalent of a pat on the back or a sympathetic nod from across the room.

OPP

OPP, pronounced as O-pee-pee. (See what I did there? Lol, ok, ok, I will mature, soon...) OPP is a lesser-known Gen Z slang, and I almost never heard anyone using it, so I'm not going to waste too much of my time on it, but I will waste yours.

OPP is short for OPPOSITION or OPPONENT, often used in street slang or rap culture to refer to a rival, enemy, or anyone who's not on your side. If someone's an OPP, they're basically the person or group you're beefing with, whether it's in a literal or metaphorical battle.

It's like when you're playing a game of basketball and that one guy on the other team is really good. He's draining three-pointers left and right, and every time he shoots, you're just like, "Man, that dude is the OPP." (I may have picked up a wrong pronunciation of the word, so it could also be just O-p) It's the ultimate shorthand for "This person is out to get me, and I'm not here for it."

In more serious contexts, OPP can refer to someone you don't trust or someone who's actively working against you—think of it as your personal villain. It's not just limited to street or rap culture, though. Anyone can be labeled an OPP if they're standing in your way or playing for the other side. Got a coworker who keeps throwing you under the bus at meetings? Yep, that's the office OPP. Or maybe it's that one person in your friend group who's always bringing negative vibes—congratulations, they've officially earned the OPP title.

And of course, if you're living in the meme universe, "OPP" is ripe for some humor. Anytime someone messes up your day—even if it's something minor—you can throw out a dramatic, "They're the OPP now." Your sibling eats the last slice of pizza? OPP. Your friend cancels plans last minute? Double OPP. It's a fun way to make light of everyday annoyances, even if your "rival" is just out here causing minor inconveniences.

But no matter how you use it, being called OPP is never a compliment. It's basically the same as being labeled "the enemy," and no one wants to be on that side of things. So, keep an eye out for your OPPS—because they're definitely out there, plotting to ruin your vibe.

Out of Pocket

This is actually a good start. If there's one Gen Z slang I want you to remember, it's this one. Out of Pocket. You can use it every time a Gen Z peep says something bizarre or something you don't understand...

OUT OF POCKET is Gen Z's way of saying someone has crossed the line, gone rogue, or just said something so wild it's in another dimension. When you hear someone say, "That was OUT OF POCKET," they're calling out behavior that's bizarre, inappropriate, or just plain crazy—something that leaves you blinking in shock, wondering, "Did they really just say that?"

Imagine this: you're all hanging out, and one of your friends suddenly drops a joke that's so edgy it's practically a knife. Everyone else is laughing politely, but you're thinking, "Whoa, that was OUT OF POCKET." Or maybe your aunt corners you at a family gathering to grill you about your love life, financial status, and every other uncomfortable topic. That level of invasion? Also OUT OF POCKET.

It's often used to describe comments or actions that are so random or offensive that they catch people off guard. If someone says something wildly inappropriate in a group chat, you can bet someone will respond with, "Wow, that's OUT OF POCKET" as a way to say, "Hey, you might wanna tone it down a notch."

But OUT OF POCKET can also be a roast for when someone's acting embarrassingly out there. If a friend decides to start freestyle rapping at 2 a.m. when no one asked for it? Yep, OUT OF POCKET. I know this was a bad and edgy example, but I am out of ideas...HELP ME HERE, will you? Thanks.

And then there's the flip side, where it's also used for people who are just plain chaotic in a fun way. Maybe they're dancing wildly at a party or pulling unexpected pranks. It's like a harmless way of saying, "They're living their best life, but also... what are they even doing?"

Next time someone gets a little OUT OF POCKET—whether it's funny, cringe, or downright savage—you'll know they've veered off the map of social norms. And hey, if you're the one acting OUT OF POCKET, own it! Sometimes, those boundary-pushing moments make for the best stories.

Owned.

Owned. Not technically a Gen Z slang, since I, a Millennial, have been using this word since before Gen Z was even around. But after talking to them, I hear it a lot, so I decided to add it. (This has absolutely NOTHING to do with making my book longer to make it look more professional. Seriously. More pages make a book look better and more legit, right? Right? Please tell me I didn't just waste all my efforts.)

Alright, back to you getting OWNED!

OWNED is the Gen Z way of saying someone just got totally, brutally, and hilariously defeated—whether in a game, argument, roast battle, or even in life. If you get OWNED, someone has metaphorically wiped the floor with you, and you have no choice but to take the L and move on. It's the digital equivalent of being knocked out cold in front of a crowd.

You're having a heated debate with a friend about who's the better artist, and they come prepared with an entire PowerPoint of your top five cringiest music choices. You have no comeback; you've been OWNED. Or maybe you try to trash-talk someone online, only for them to hit back with a response so cutting it could slice through steel. The crowd goes wild, and you're left staring at your screen like, "Well, that escalated quickly..."

OWNED can also be used in gaming, where it's practically a way of life. If someone goes on a winning streak, completely demolishing every player in sight, you're watching a masterclass in OWNING the competition. And let's be real—if you're on the losing end, you just got OWNED. (As you usually do)

There's a certain joy in using OWNED as a comeback, too. If someone tries to come for you with a weak insult, and you snap back with a one-liner that has everyone laughing, you've OWNED them. Or, if someone's bragging about something you know is false, just raise an eyebrow and casually say, "Well, OWNED." It's like letting them know they just walked into their own doom. If you're ever on the receiving end of an OWNING, take it like a champ. We've all been there. And if you're the one doing the OWNING, enjoy the moment—because there's nothing quite like landing that perfect burn that leaves everyone else scrambling to recover.

Periodt

Did you notice the T at the end of the word "PERIODT"? Well, good for you, because I didn't notice it when I was talking to Gen Z. It was only after I saw their text messages that I asked what it was, and here's what I found out.

PERIODT is the ultimate mic drop in Gen Z slang. When someone says PERIODT, they're making it clear that the discussion is OVER, the point has been made, and there's absolutely nothing left to add. Think of it like the exclamation point of spoken language. Whether you're laying down some hard truths, declaring your favorite snack to be the best of all time, or just shutting down someone's argument with finality, you wrap it up with PERIODT for that extra punch.

At this point, you're probably growing tired of the overuse of the word "*ULTIMATE*" in every example or explanation. Well, guess what? I'll add even more of it, just to make you angrier. Periodt. But if it makes you happy, you win this one. You win this one, dear friend.

Let's continue, say your friend tries to argue that pineapple doesn't belong on pizza. (This is just an example, Italians, so please lower your spaghetti guns.) You hit them with, "Pineapple on pizza is delicious, PERIODT." Boom. Argument settled, whether they agree or not. The added "t" at the end is what gives it extra force. It's like saying, "I'm so right that you'll need a whole committee to argue against me, but good luck with that."

PERIODT can also be a great way to hype up a friend. Imagine someone just slayed their outfit, aced a presentation, or roasted someone who totally deserved it. You hit them with, "You did that, PERIODT," letting them know they owned the moment, and there's no questioning it.

The next time you need to shut down a conversation, hype yourself up, or add some OOMPH to a statement, throw in a PERIODT and let the world know there's no more room for debate.

Pick me (Girl/Guy)

What do you call a Gen Z without internet? A lost connection.

Crickets

Now that I have your attention, let's get into this Gen Z slang.

PICK ME is the **ultimate** (haha, F*ck yeah, I love doing whatever I want with my book.) term for someone who's trying way too hard to stand out by putting themselves above others—usually in a way that screams, "Look at how different and special I am!" (Ah, sh*t, I'm a pick-me girl, aren't I? Oh well, f*ck it.)

A PICK ME person is that one friend who will bend over backward to impress or appeal, often by putting down others or acting like they're "not like other people." It's almost like they're saying, "Please choose me as the most unique one of the bunch!" in a way that's A BIT MUCH.

Imagine someone in a group chat saying, "I don't even care about looks; I'm all about personality." Or they'll go, "I'm just one of the guys—I hate drama, unlike other girls." Cue the collective sigh, because most of the time, these statements are less about being real and more about fishing for attention or compliments. It's that feeling of "Oh, you think you're better than everyone else, huh?" with a side-eye.

PICK ME behavior doesn't always have to be loud, either. Sometimes it's subtle, like a person who claims they're the only one in the group who "just can't stand social media" but makes a huge deal out of saying so... on social media. Or they might throw in lines like, "Oh, I'm just so low-maintenance, unlike SOME people," as if they're trying to score points for being effortlessly cool and down-to-earth.

It's not necessarily evil, but it's definitely cringe. And calling it out is a way of saying, "We see what you're doing, and honestly, it's a bit transparent." So, if you catch yourself going for that "I'm so unique" gold star, just remember: there's no shame in being authentically you without the PICK ME energy. And if someone else is on a roll with their PICK ME statements? Just grab some popcorn, because it's usually quite the performance.

Pluh

Imagine if eyerolling had a word? (Actually, it does have a word: it's called eyerolling.) Well, GEN Z created a word for it. (Like I said, there is a word for eyerolling, but for some reason, GEN Z made a new one.) That would be PLUH.

PLUH is Gen Z's way of giving a giant, WHATEVER-level eyeroll. It's short for "player hater," and if you're calling someone a PLUH, you're letting them know they're bringing down the vibe, possibly out of jealousy or just plain sourness. It's like calling someone out for being a walking raincloud—no one invited their negative energy, yet here they are, shading the entire scene.

Picture this: someone walks in, and before anyone can even breathe, they're already talking about how everyone's favorite show is "overrated" or that the new pizza place in town "isn't all that." This person? CERTIFIED PLUH. It's the kind of person who seems to THRIVE on pointing out flaws, finding fault with things just for the sake of it. Calling them a PLUH is the quick way of saying, "Yeah, we see you, killjoy."

Now, a PLUH isn't always in-your-face either. Sometimes, it's the subtle hater energy that really seals the deal. Like when someone side-eyes your playlist and says, "I guess that's fine... if you like mainstream stuff." Oof. That's some PLUH energy if we've ever seen it. Or, when you're hyping up your plans and they hit you with, "Cool, if you're into basic things." It's like they couldn't just let people enjoy things, so they have to sprinkle a little shade everywhere they go.

The funniest part about a PLUH? They're often convinced they're being deep and edgy, as if they're the only ones brave enough to "tell it like it is." But to the rest of us, it just sounds like, "Yawn. Do you ever let yourself have fun?" So, next time someone's acting like a PLUH, go ahead and hit them with a "pluh alert!" You'll either shut them down or, at the very least, make them rethink that endless supply of negativity.

And if you ever find yourself being the PLUH, maybe try not being a professional downer for five minutes. It might just change your life!

Pookie.

Gone are the days of "BAE" or "BABE." Now, it's all about POOKIE. Boy oh boy, I wonder what future generations have in store for us. Maybe Gen Alpha will start using COOKIE as a term of endearment. Anyhow, let's dive into POOKIE, since this is a GEN Z lingo dictionary.

POOKIE is Gen Z's way of affectionately referring to someone in their life who's cute, endearing, and maybe a little clueless in a charming way. Think of it as a blend of "sweetheart" and "adorable goof." When someone calls you POOKIE, they're putting you in that special category of "too precious for this world" but also maybe a little clueless. It's like calling someone a cuddly stuffed animal with questionable street smarts.

Imagine someone in your group chat who's always getting into ridiculous situations, like accidentally sending a voice memo of themselves singing to their boss or spilling coffee on themselves right before a big date. Instead of saying, "Bless your heart," you just go, "Aww, POOKIE!" It's part sympathy, part amusement, and mostly endearing.

But sometimes, POOKIE can also be used with a hint of mockery—especially if someone's acting overly sensitive, confused, or downright cringey. Imagine that friend who texts at 2 a.m. in a crisis because they accidentally liked their ex's 2012 Instagram post while stalking. You hit them with, "Oh no, POOKIE," as a lighthearted way of roasting them for their own little disaster.

Of course, not everyone's worthy of the POOKIE title. It's reserved for those lovable souls who, despite their mess-ups, are just too cute and innocent to be mad at. So if you've been dubbed a POOKIE, take it as both a compliment and a reminder: you're loved, but you also might be one "whoops" away from wrapping yourself in bubble wrap.

So, POOKIE, if you reached to this point, congratz.

POOKIE.

Queen

Sorry, Kings, but this word is for us. It's the one word that we, women, can use to make ourselves feel better. (INSERT A SMILEY FACE HERE)

Now, let's get to the explanation so you can understand it better.

QUEEN is the internet's royal title for anyone who's absolutely slaying it—whether they're acing their life goals, delivering killer comebacks, or just radiating so much confidence that everyone else feels inspired (or a little jealous). When someone calls you a QUEEN, they're basically bowing down to your excellence, saying, "Yes, we see you, and you are CRUSHING it." It's a crown without the weight, a compliment without comparison.

A QUEEN doesn't have to wear an actual crown; she probably wouldn't be caught dead in one, actually. (This is not a Queen Elizabeth joke. I repeat, this is not a joke, just an example.)

A QUEEN is someone who is busy running things—whether that's her career, her friendships, or even just a flawless makeup routine that makes everyone else question their life choices. If you see someone winning in every possible way and radiating that "I got this" energy, you're looking at a QUEEN. And don't even try to mess with her because she can roast with such elegance that you'll thank her for it.

Now, QUEEN can also be the rallying cry for someone who's standing up for themselves, breaking barriers, or just being unapologetically themselves. Imagine your friend who finally quit that job that was sucking her soul dry or dumped that terrible ex—she's a QUEEN. Or someone who just nailed a karaoke rendition of a Beyoncé song with zero shame? QUEEN behavior.

And let's not forget the joy of using QUEEN as the ultimate hype-up for your friends: "Yes, QUEEN! Get that A on your final exam!" or "Queen, you better show up to that interview like they already hired you!" It's a full endorsement, a reminder that they're capable of ROYAL-LEVEL greatness.

If you still didn't get it from the very first paragraph, the male version of QUEEN is KING. Yes, there's also a word for you boys. Rejoice.

Ratio

If you don't use Twitter/X or Instagram, you can skip this, because this GEN Z slang is only used and understood in terms of replies and comments. If you DO use social media (may Heaven help you), then let's get down to business to defeat the slangs!

RATIO is the internet's version of saying, "I just won this argument, and the numbers prove it." It's used primarily on social media, especially Twitter/X, when someone replies to a post, and their reply gets more likes, retweets, or engagement than the original post. If you get RATIOED, it means the internet masses have decided that your take wasn't it, and someone else's response has completely overshadowed yours. It's like a digital smackdown, backed up with cold, hard numbers.

Imagine you tweet something controversial or just wildly unpopular, and within minutes, someone replies with a witty clapback that's getting way more love than your original post. Congratulations, you've been RATIOED. It's not just a loss—it's a loss so public and quantifiable that it feels like you're being dunked on by the entire internet.

Now, it's not always brutal. Sometimes RATIO is just a game, like when someone tweets "Ratio me if pineapple on pizza is amazing" or "Like this if you agree with me, and reply to RATIO me if you don't." In these cases, it's an invitation to RATIO, a way to see what the majority really thinks, even if it's a friendly debate. But in most cases, getting RATIOED is the online equivalent of having tomatoes thrown at you—especially if you posted a hot take that went over like a lead balloon.

And let's be real: sometimes people try to RATIO each other for fun or as a joke, adding fuel to an online roast. If you're feeling bold and think you can clap back harder than the original post, you might reply with "Ratio" as a one-word power move. It's like saying, "I bet I'll get more love than you for this," and it's the perfect setup for an online showdown.

The next time you see a RATIO happening, grab your popcorn—it's the internet's way of keeping score, one like at a time. And if you ever get RATIOED? Take the L with grace, because let's be honest, we all fall to the RATIO eventually.

Red Flag

Yes, this is exactly what you think it is. This Slang has been used before Gen Z, and Gen Z uses it as well, and hopefully, future generations will use it too. But if you have lived under a rock for the past 6,000 years, here is an explanation.

A RED FLAG is the internet's way of saying, "Warning! Danger ahead!" It's like seeing a flashing neon sign over someone's head that says, "Proceed with caution, unless you enjoy chaos." A RED FLAG signals those behaviors or traits that scream, "This might end badly." If you're spotting RED FLAGS, you're noticing the little clues that someone—or something—might not be all sunshine and good vibes. Think of it as the relationship version of a flashing "do not enter" sign.

Imagine you're chatting with someone who casually mentions they don't believe in texting back within a week, or someone says, "Yeah, I don't really have any close friends." Both of these are RED FLAGS so loud they practically echo. It's like saying, "Hey, I come with warning labels—ignore them at your own risk."

The beauty of RED FLAGS is how they've taken over social media as a fun way to call out things that are harmless, questionable, or downright disastrous. Your friend orders pineapple on pizza? Red Flag. Someone says they've never seen SHREK? Red Flag. Your crush tells you their "last situationship didn't work out because EVERYONE'S CRAZY EXCEPT ME"? Mega Red Flag. It's a way of saying, "Watch out!" with a wink, and sometimes with genuine concern.

But let's be real, we all have our own RED FLAGS. Maybe you have a secret fondness for dad jokes, an ALARMINGLY large collection of expired condiments, or a tendency to binge-watch reality TV until 3 a.m. The key is spotting RED FLAGS that are legit deal-breakers versus the ones that are more like quirks. Because while some RED FLAGS are cute, some are the warning signs that make you want to sprint in the opposite direction.

When you're spotting RED FLAGS, remember: it's all fun and games until you're wading knee-deep in them. Choose wisely, or at least have a good escape plan ready!

Rizz

Let's play a little game. Can you find the times I used the word RIZZ in the previous examples? I'll give you a few minutes to go back and read this book again (up to this point of course, but—you figured that out yourself, right? Right? Ok, good.)

RIZZ is Gen Z's version of charisma, charm, and smooth-talking swagger, all rolled into one. If you've got RIZZ, you've got that mysterious ability to effortlessly attract, flirt, or just make someone feel like they're the most interesting person in the room. It's a level of game that's part confidence, part mystery, and part "Oh, this old thing?" attitude. When someone says, "He's got RIZZ," they mean he could probably walk into a room and turn heads without even trying.

Having RIZZ isn't about throwing out cheesy pick-up lines or trying too hard—it's about having a vibe so strong that people just WANT to be around you. Imagine someone who strolls in with a casual, laid-back confidence, drops a quick, funny comment, and suddenly has everyone laughing and leaning in to hear more. That's pure RIZZ at work.

And then, of course, there's the endless entertainment of RIZZ variations: you might hear about people with UNSPOKEN RIZZ, meaning they don't even have to say a word to get attention, or W-RIZZ, meaning they're scoring wins left and right with their charm. On the flip side, there's L-RIZZ, which is essentially anti-rizz—attempts at charm that fall flatter than a pancake. If you're trying to flirt and keep hearing crickets in response, sorry, but that's L-RIZZ in action.

To have RIZZ is to embody the smooth, low-key confidence that's magnetic but subtle. It's the type of energy that makes people want to be around you without knowing quite why. And if you're blessed with RIZZ? Use it wisely, because let's be real, not everyone can handle the charm overload.

Ok, now, if you actually did go back and reread the book looking for the word RIZZ, I'm sorry to prank you, but I never used it. Sorry for wasting your time (actually, I'm not sorry at all).

Roasted

You might be wondering, isn't ROASTED the same as GETTING OWNED? Well, technically, yes, they're very similar. But I'm not here to skip a word just because it overlaps with another slang. No, I'm here to explain ALL the slangs I learned after living under the bridge with Gen Z people. (And if enough people buy my book, I might even afford a cardboard box over my head—ah, I love shameless self-promotion.)

Now, back to ROASTED!

If you haven't been ROASTED before, congratulations—you've either been living under a rock or you're too pure for this world. In Gen Z slang, getting ROASTED means being hilariously, brutally, and maybe even embarrassingly called out in a way that leaves no room for argument. When you're ROASTED, you're not just lightly teased; you're taken down with such pinpoint accuracy that it almost becomes an art form. Think of it as verbal BBQ: slow-cooked, extra crispy, and served with zero mercy.

Imagine this: you show up with an outfit that you thought was fire, only for your friend to hit you with, "BRO, ARE WE GOING CAMPING? BECAUSE YOU'RE DEFINITELY OUT HERE LOOKING LIKE A TENT." That's a roast. Or you make a big claim, like, "I'M DEFINITELY GOING TO START WORKING OUT," and someone just gives you a look and says, "YEAH, LIKE YOU DID LAST JANUARY?" Burn level: expert.

Roasting is all about the fine balance of being funny and slightly ruthless but not so far that you ruin friendships (usually). A good roast will have everyone laughing—even the person getting roasted—because it's based on a kernel of truth that's impossible to deny. Roasts are meant to be memorable, so they tend to sting just enough to make you think twice before bringing that topic up again. But if you're dishing it out, be ready to take it. Gen Z loves a roast session, and what goes around, definitely comes back around. If you're coming for someone, just be prepared—you might be next on the grill. Next time you roast someone, go for the perfect balance of funny and just barely too much. Because when it's done right, there's nothing better than a good, spicy roast.

Salty

Now, if you're not familiar with this one, it might sound like something you'd sprinkle on your fries, but in Gen Z slang, it has nothing to do with seasoning.

SALTY describes someone who's bitter, annoyed, or just straight-up grumpy about something. Think of it as a sassier way of saying, "YOU'RE MAD, BRO." If you've ever been that person who's still ranting about losing a game three days later, congrats—you're officially SALTY.

And if you're sitting here thinking, "I'VE NEVER BEEN SALTY," let me burst your bubble, because that just sounds like something a SALTY person would say. Everyone gets salty sometimes, whether you want to admit it or not. Like, remember when your coworker got credit for your idea, and you sat there clapping but secretly wanted to flip the whole table? Yeah, that's SALTY.

Being SALTY can even become a personality trait. We all know that one person who can't let anything go. You forget to text them back? They'll bring it up three weeks later. Accidentally step on their shoes? Prepare to hear about it every time you see them. It's almost impressive, really, how some people can hold onto the tiniest slights and let them simmer until they're seasoned with maximum saltiness.

The best example is being SALTY after purchasing a book that makes fun of you for not knowing Gen Z slang... oh no... never mind, please ignore this paragraph.

The beauty of SALTY is that it's almost universal. It doesn't matter who you are—everyone gets a little salty now and then. Whether it's missing out on a promotion, getting called out in a group chat, or realizing someone unfollowed you on social media, life is full of tiny, annoying moments that turn us into temporary salt mines. Embrace your saltiness! Sometimes, it's just your inner pettiness shining through, and honestly, that's what makes life interesting.

After all, what's a world without a little SALT?

Savage

Let's give credit where credit is due. Unlike us Boomers and Millennials, Gen Z peeps are very straightforward and bold. If they want something, they'll go for it. We tend to be a little shy to ask or lack confidence at times, but not these kids. These kids are SAVAGE. What does it mean? Well here I go.

SAVAGE is a CHEF'S KISS of Gen Z slang. When something or someone is called SAVAGE, they've gone beyond the limits of polite society and into the territory of brutal honesty, sharp comebacks, or bold moves that leave everyone else either gasping or cracking up. It's the kind of behavior that's ruthlessly honest and maybe a little harsh, but undeniably impressive. Think of it as being a modern-day gladiator—but instead of wielding a sword, you're dropping truth bombs and devastating comebacks. BASED CHAD.

Let say someone posts a painfully obvious selfie with the caption, "UGH, I LOOK SO BAD." And instead of politely ignoring it, you swoop in with, "YEAH, BUT YOU POSTED IT ANYWAY, HUH?" Bam. Savage. Or maybe your friend shows up late for the third time in a row, and instead of a mild, "HEY, NO WORRIES," you hit them with, "GLAD YOU COULD JOIN US SLOWPOKE." That's not just honesty—that's SAVAGE honesty.

Now, don't get too excited just yet. SAVAGE isn't about being mean for no reason. There's an art to it; it's all about timing, delivery, and knowing just how far to go without crossing the line into plain rudeness. It's more about saying what everyone else is thinking but would never dare to say. If you can pull it off, people will respect you for it. But if you miss the mark? You'll just come off as bitter and, let's be honest, a little desperate.

And let's be real—if you're thinking, "OH, I'M TOTALLY SAVAGE," you're probably not. True SAVAGES don't need to declare it. They let their actions do the talking, while everyone else just stands there in awe, wondering how they had the guts to say what they did. Before you start dropping your SAVAGE one-liners all over the place, ask yourself if you've really got the chops for it. It's a lifestyle choice, and not everyone can handle it. Go forth, but tread carefully—because not everyone's ready for the SAVAGE side of you.

Schooled

Oh, so you want to know about SCHOOLED? Well, buckle up, because it's time for a lesson! When a GEN Z says they got SCHOOLED, it means they just got hit with a serious reality check. Maybe they got shown up, put in their place, or just learned a hard truth they didn't see coming. Being SCHOOLED is a polite way of saying someone got totally outsmarted, outdone, or absolutely roasted, often in a way that's just embarrassing enough to sting but not enough to call an ambulance.

Let say you're feeling confident about your ping-pong skills, talking a big game, only for your friend to come in and annihilate you in front of everyone. They didn't just beat you—they SCHOOLED you. Or maybe you tried to flex your "knowledge" on a topic, only for someone to hit you with actual facts that leave you speechless. Boom. SCHOOLED. It's that moment when you realize, maybe, just maybe, you were out of your depth and someone else was holding the syllabus the whole time.

And here's the kicker: getting SCHOOLED isn't bad! It is very, very bad. Sometimes it's a reality check that you might actually NEED. But let's be honest, it's still pretty funny if it happens to someone else. When you feel like you're ready to step up and show off, just be prepared. Because if you're not careful, you might be the one getting SCHOOLED—and trust me, nobody forgets when that happens.

Secure the Bag

Gucci or Hermès? Well, it doesn't matter 'cause both are a success. (*Sigh*, my attempt at writing poems is ICK, and I know it. Just pretend that it sounded good, okay?)

SECURE THE BAG might sound like you're guarding your groceries or your purse, but it's actually a phrase in Gen Z slang.

To SECURE THE BAG means to lock down success, win the prize, or make sure you're getting what's rightfully yours—especially when it comes to money, career goals, or any kind of personal achievement. It's the slang version of GET THAT BREAD, but with a touch more swagger.

You've just aced a job interview and walked out with a killer salary offer. That's SECURING THE BAG. Or maybe you found a way to turn your side hustle into a full-time gig—SECURED THAT BAG, my friend. It's about hustling and making sure you're maximizing every opportunity, stacking up those wins, and not letting anything stand in the way of your goals.

But listen, not everyone is cut out to SECURE THE BAG. Some people are too busy scrolling social media or binge-watching shows to focus on actually making moves. If that sounds like you, maybe it's time for a reality check. SECURING THE BAG isn't about hoping for success to magically fall into your lap—it's about putting in the work, grinding it out, and not letting yourself get sidetracked by nonsense.

And before you go around saying you're out here "securing the bag," make sure you're actually doing it. Talk is cheap, but the BAG isn't. If you're serious about it, get focused, get determined, and start checking off those goals. And if you're just using it to sound cool? Well, good luck with that—because you've got a long way to go before you're actually SECURING anything except a participation trophy.

Sheesh

Oh, sheesh! I almost forgot about it... Well, this one is going to be a short one, isn't it?

SHEESH. This isn't just a word—it's a full-on vibe. SHEESH is the verbal equivalent of your jaw hitting the floor. It's that exclamation for when something is so hype, so outrageous, or so flex-worthy that you can't just say, "Wow, that's neat." No, no. You've gotta hit it with the drawn-out, "SHEEESH!"—preferably with a high-pitched, dramatic tone that makes everyone turn their heads and feel the hype. It's like a compliment, a gasp, and a virtual fire emoji all rolled into one.

But listen, not just anyone can pull off SHEESH. If you're trying it out and you sound more like an off-brand dad or a confused teacher, you're doing it wrong. A true SHEESH has style, has flair, and, ideally, a bit of that dramatic upward inflection, like "SHEEESH!" It's practically musical. Get it right, and people will feel that hype. Get it wrong, and they'll just feel... awkward.

And don't even think about dropping a SHEESH on something low-key or unimpressive. This isn't the word you whip out when your coffee order is correct. SHEESH is reserved for only the most EPIC moments of hype, drama, and jaw-dropping scenes. If you can't find that level of excitement, maybe just sit this one out.

If you feel that SHEESH urge is coming on, ask yourself, "IS THIS THE LEGENDARY MOMENT?" If yes, then go all in. But if it's just your friend showing you their new phone case, please spare us. Remember: with great SHEESH comes great reSHEESHponsibility.

Ok, I'll see myself out...

Sigma

Now, if you're curious about SIGMA in the Gen Z lingo, get ready, because this one goes deep. (...but not as deep as your...no, I'm not making that joke. I don't need your mama showing up at my doorstep.)

SIGMA refers to a type of personality—think of it as a mythical creature in the world of social archetypes. A SIGMA MALE (or female, because SIGMA energy knows no bounds) is someone who marches to the beat of their own drum, doesn't care about traditional hierarchies, and doesn't need anyone's approval. They're essentially the "lone wolf" who looks at all the social ranks—Alpha, Beta, etc.—and just shrugs. They don't play by the rules because, to them, the rules are irrelevant. They're off doing their own thing, living their best life, unbothered by society's expectations.

Imagine the SIGMA as the person in high school who didn't need to hang with the popular kids or join any cliques. They were just... there, mysterious, possibly wearing all black, showing up only when they felt like it. They were cool, but not because they tried to be. If someone said, "HEY, YOU COMING TO THE PARTY?" they'd probably just give you a smirk and walk off into the sunset without a word. SIGMA ENERGY is all about independence, confidence, and a little bit of mystery—and a whole lot of, "I don't need you, but you definitely need me."

Of course, in typical Gen Z fashion, SIGMA has also become a bit of a meme. People love to exaggerate the whole SIGMA persona, making it look like they're some kind of unfeeling, emotionally detached superhero. You'll see jokes about SIGMA behavior where someone ignores all messages, cuts ties with everyone, or ditches societal norms altogether. It's like the modern-day brooding antihero. If you're really out here answering texts within five minutes and attending every social event, let's be honest—you're more of a BETA pretending to be SIGMA.

Go forth, lone wolf. But remember, SIGMA isn't just a word; it's a whole vibe. You can't fake SIGMA—you either have it, or you're out here grinding to get it, probably while watching SIGMA motivation videos on repeat.

SIMP

I can't believe we've actually reached this point. You're actually simping for me, aren't you? Or do you just really like my book? I'll be damned... Thank you. Anyway, you might not have noticed—or maybe you did—how I subtly slipped in the word SIMP. Haha, gotcha.

Simp! (Yes, you are, and you know it. WINK WINK Don't tell your SO about it.)

It is a term that's been through the social media wringer and has emerged as Gen Z's playful roast for anyone who might be just a LITTLE TOO NICE (read: over-the-top, almost embarrassingly nice) toward someone they're interested in. A SIMP is someone who's so infatuated with someone that they'll go to almost absurd lengths to win their favor, often without getting much in return. Imagine someone paying $5 for a text-back, handing over endless compliments like it's a charity drive, or dedicating all their time to someone who barely remembers their last name. That's SIMP behavior in a nutshell.

But let's not get it twisted—SIMP isn't all bad. There's a charm to being devoted and showing someone you care, but SIMPING takes it to a whole new level. It's like dialing up the admiration to the point where it becomes almost desperate. And let's face it, desperation isn't exactly cute. If you're out here liking every single post, commenting "perfect" on every picture, and sending thoughtful good morning texts that never get a reply, you might want to reassess the balance of power here. Spoiler: you're not exactly WINNING it.

Of course, SIMP has become a meme, which means people will call you a simp just for holding the door open for someone. Got someone you're genuinely interested in? Congrats, you're a SIMP. Spend an extra second talking to your crush? You're SIMPING. It's less about WHAT you do and more about whether or not you're TRYING TOO HARD. The line between respectful admiration and full-on simping is thin—and Gen Z will let you know the minute you cross it.

But hey, if you're gonna simp, own it. Everyone's been a SIMP at one point or another, and it's part of the game. Just remember: if you're putting in all this effort for someone who barely gives you a like, maybe you're simping just a LITTLE too hard. And if you're out here calling yourself a SIMP proudly, at least you're self-aware. Because in the end, the real SIMP move is going all in and forgetting to respect yourself in the process. If you're gonna simp, do it with pride—but maybe sprinkle in a little self-respect while you're at it.

And no, SIMP is not the antonym for SIGMA. The antonym for Sigma is BETA. A person you see in the mirror. Oof roasted.

Skibidi

If you don't know or haven't heard this word before, please save yourself and skip this slang. But if you're willing to sacrifice your sanity, then proceed with caution.

SKIBIDI!

If you're wondering what on Earth this term is doing in Gen Z slang, welcome to the weird, wacky world of internet culture. SKIBIDI originally comes from the viral TikTok dance trend that's rooted in an ultra-catchy, absurdist song and dance combo. We're talking about random dance moves, bobbing heads, and chaotic, looping music that just sticks in your brain for no reason. It's catchy, it's bizarre, and somehow, it's a whole vibe.

The full SKIBIDI phenomenon has gone beyond just a sound on TikTok. We now have SKIBIDI TOILET, a hilarious and surreal animated series on YouTube where toilets with human heads face off against camera-headed people in an epic battle of, well…whatever. It's like a fever dream you didn't ask for but can't stop watching. And the best part? No one fully understands what's going on, but everyone's here for the randomness of it all.

But SKIBIDI isn't just about the series or the dance moves—it's become a whole attitude, a shorthand for chaotic energy that's half-meme, half-bizarre performance art.

When someone says "Skibidi," they're leaning into a kind of random and dumb fun, the kind that doesn't need a logical explanation. It's as if Gen Z looked at the concept of "troll humor" and thought, "LET'S CRANK THIS UP TO ELEVEN."

In short, the shortest of short, Skibidi is basically nonsense. Yes, I did waste your time.

YOU'RE welcome.

Slaps

Come here, lemme slap yo face, yah?

Ok, I'll stop. (I'm trying to be funny for your sake) But Gen Z slang doesn't mean what you think it means—in fact, it actually means something good.

If you hear that something SLAPS, don't go checking for injuries—it's actually a huge compliment. When something SLAPS, it means it's so good it practically hits you in the face with how amazing it is. This term is mostly used for music, but it's versatile enough to apply to anything with serious impact: food, movies, outfits, you name it. If a song SLAPS, it's one you'll be blasting on repeat; if a taco SLAPS, you're coming back for seconds, maybe thirds.

Let's say your friend shows you a new playlist, and the first track just hits you with that perfect beat drop. You're not just saying, "I LIKE IT." No, that would be boring. You're saying, "YO, THIS SLAPS!"—because just "liking" it doesn't capture the sheer force of its greatness. It's the kind of music that makes you do that little head-bob or put on your best stank face because, honestly, it's too good not to.

SLAPS is also reserved for anything that goes HARD, anything that delivers way more than you expected. A song can SLAP, but so can a meme that's perfectly relatable or a TikTok video that's so funny you spit out your drink. It's like the cultural stamp of approval that says, "THIS IS IT; THIS IS THE GOOD STUFF."

Find something that SLAPS, and make sure everyone knows it. Just try not to overuse it—because let's face it, if EVERYTHING slaps, does anything really slap at all? Keep it selective, and let SLAPS hold onto its power.

Slay

Do you know how many Gen Z peeps I had to slay just to finish this book? That's right—zero. Those kids are impossible to slay. Oh, you thought I meant "slay" in the cool way? Nope, I meant SLAY, as in actually slay... Confused? Good. Prepare to get **schooled** on one of Gen Z's highest forms of praise.

When you SLAY, you're absolutely crushing it—you're looking amazing, acting with confidence, and just radiating that effortless MAIN CHARACTER ENERGY. SLAY is like the gold star of compliments, used when someone is looking or doing something so flawlessly that everyone else might as well go home. SLAY doesn't just mean you did well; it means you OWNED it.

Imagine this: your friend shows up to a party dressed to the nines, makeup on point, hair flowing like it was styled by the gods themselves. You don't just say, "You look nice." Oh no, you say, "YOU SLAY!" Or maybe they just aced a big presentation or served up a comeback that left everyone speechless. In that moment, SLAY is the only word that does justice to the sheer greatness on display. It's the word for moments where "good" or even "great" fall short of the kind of perfection they're achieving.

But of course, SLAY has taken on meme status, too. People use it for just about anything now, often in an ironic way. Did you manage to show up to work on time? SLAY. Make it through a painfully awkward conversation with your crush without crumbling? SLAY. Ate a salad instead of pizza? ABSOLUTE SLAY. It's a whole vibe of hyping yourself or someone else up for even the smallest wins, because let's face it—we're all just out here trying our best.

When you're out there hustling, handling business, or just looking good doing the bare minimum, feel free to claim your SLAY. Whether it's an over-the-top slay or a humble, low-key slay, own it. Because if you're slaying, everyone around you better take notes.

Did I SLAY this explanation or what?

And, by the way, no Gen Z were harmed in the making of this book. (Well, not all of them at least—some miraculously survived.)

Stan

I know you might be thinking I'm referring to a person named Stan, but nope, that's not it. However, you're definitely going to laugh when you find out what this slang actually means. So here's your 10-minute warning—prepare yourself, because when it clicks, you'll probably laugh even harder.

Welcome to the world of unapologetic, all-consuming fandom. To STAN someone means to be their biggest, most loyal, slightly obsessive fan. It's like saying, "I'm not just a fan—I'd defend this person like it's my life's mission." A STAN goes above and beyond the regular levels of admiration; it's fan support on steroids. And yes, it's all thanks to Eminem's infamous song "Stan," where he portrayed an obsessed fan who wrote unhinged letters. But don't worry, these days STAN is way more lighthearted (usually, but not always).

If you say, "I stan Beyoncé," you're not just saying you like her music. No, you're saying you'd sell your left leg for a concert ticket, know every lyric by heart, and have a mental PowerPoint ready for anyone who dares question her greatness.

STAN culture means passionately supporting and hyping up your fave, often in online spaces. Got a favorite artist, influencer, or even a TikTok chef? You're probably part of their STAN army, liking, sharing, and defending them online like you're on payroll.

STAN can also be used as a verb. Did your friend finally binge-watch that show you've been pushing on them for weeks? You'll probably say, "FINALLY, YOU STAN." And if you're saying "WE STAN" about something, it means it has achieved universal approval status. In short, stanning is next-level fandom—it's when you've gone from casual fan to unofficial hype person.

But here's the warning label: stanning can get INTENSE. Stan culture online has become a battlefield where stans fiercely defend their favorites and sometimes even start fan wars, just know there's a point where dedication turns into obsession—and Gen Z knows exactly how to walk that line.

You must be wondering, "Wait, that wasn't funny at all. Why did you make me prepare?" Well, I'm sorry—it WAS funny to me. Now that I've read it 69 times, I'm starting to realize... maybe it's not THAT funny.

Snatched

Correct. You are absolutely correct. The best kind of correct. Snatched is GEN Z slang, and it does mean…stealing.

(Inhales and prepears my throat to sound EPIC.)

WRONG.

This is not what SNATCHED means. It's Gen Z's stylish way of saying that something looks flawless, on point, and downright enviable.If you've got a look or an outfit that's SNATCHED, it means it's put together so perfectly that it looks like it was pulled straight from a high-fashion runway. In short, SNATCHED is the ultimate compliment for someone who's slaying the game with their appearance. You didn't just get dressed; you showed up and owned it.

Typically, you'll hear SNATCHED used to describe someone's body, makeup, or overall look. "GIRL, YOUR WAIST IS SNATCHED," or "THAT CONTOUR IS SNATCHED" are the kinds of things you'll hear when someone has nailed their look with precision and skill. It's almost like saying that their style or figure looks so flawless that it's been "snatched" right out of a magazine.

But here's the thing: SNATCHED isn't just for the "natural beauty" moments. It's often used to appreciate all the hard work that goes into the LOOK. We're talking about that waist-trainer level of dedication, makeup techniques that should be considered fine art, and clothing choices that could make fashion designers applaud. SNATCHED celebrates the drama, the flair, and the over-the-top level of effort it takes to look that good.

If someone tells you you're SNATCHED, you can go ahead and bask in that praise because it's well-earned. You're not just looking good—you're looking next-level, flawlessly executed, take-a-picture-and-frame-it good. Just remember, if you're gonna be SNATCHED, you better be ready to turn heads, because this is not a term for the casual looks. It's for those moments when you're serving so hard that people have no choice but to stop and stare.

SUS

Remember the slang DELULU? Remember I said that Gen Z peeps use that slang because they didn't want to spell out the entire word DELUSIONAL? Well, SUS is the same idea—it's short for the word SUSPICIOUS. Because, you know, Gen Z wants to shorten everything.

This little three-letter word packs a punch in Gen Z slang, and it's all about suspicion. If someone or something is SUS, it means they're acting suspicious, shady, or just plain fishy.

SUS is the verbal side-eye, the one-word callout that hints someone's up to no good—or at least, something weird. Imagine someone being secretive, acting out of character, or doing something that just doesn't sit right. That's textbook SUS.

SUS first blew up in gaming culture, specifically from the game AMONG US,(Not that you've ever played a video game.) where players would call out each other as "SUS" when they suspected someone of being the imposter (aka, the one trying to sabotage everyone else). Now, it's everywhere. Got a friend who suddenly doesn't want to show you their phone screen? SUS. Someone giving a way-too-detailed excuse about why they couldn't make it to the party? SUS. Or, say, your crush likes your Instagram story at 3 a.m.? Yep, that's a little SUS, too.

What makes SUS such a hit is that it's a perfect way to call people out without going all-in on accusations. You're not saying they're guilty, but you're not totally buying what they're selling, either. You're just raising that little red flag in the form of a single word. So next time you see someone acting a little off, feel free to throw a "SUS" their way. It's the Gen Z way of saying, "I'M WATCHING YOU."

Take the W/Take the L

TAKE THE W and TAKE THE L—two phrases that might just be Gen Z's favorite ways to talk about winning and losing, but with a little more style (and attitude). This is the only slang (if you even consider it slang) that was actually easy for me to start using.

Take the W: The W stands for WIN, and TAKING THE W means scoring a victory, achieving something great, or just generally coming out on top. If someone tells you to TAKE THE W, it means to embrace that success, enjoy the moment, and maybe even brag a little. You might hear it in a sports setting ("WE TOTALLY TOOK THE W AT THE GAME LAST NIGHT") or just as a way to say, "Congrats, you nailed it." Got an A on a tough exam? Take the W. Just landed that job? Definitely take the W!

Take the L: On the flip side, TAKE THE L (L for LOSS) means to accept a defeat or failure. But it's more than just losing—it's about shrugging it off, learning from it, and moving on. "YEAH, I TOTALLY FAILED THAT PRESENTATION, BUT I'LL TAKE THE L AND DO BETTER NEXT TIME." It's like saying, "Alright, I messed up, but it's cool. I'm moving forward." Taking the L is about owning up to the setback, without wallowing in it.

And Gen Z likes to throw these phrases around humorously, too. Maybe you trip in public—your friends might just say, "TAKE THE L." Or you win a silly argument? "GO AHEAD, TAKE THE W." They're versatile phrases for adding a little flair to life's ups and downs.

Anyone who bought this book TAKES THE W (or the L)

TAXED

We all hate taxes—always have, always will.

FUDGE THE TAXES.

In Gen Z slang, TAXED means feeling completely drained, exhausted, or overwhelmed. It's that point where you've hit your limit and have absolutely nothing left in the tank.

Is it similar to COOKED? Kinda yes, but no. In Gen Z slang, both are used to describe situations where someone or something is in a bad state, but they have different nuances. "COOKED" is more about being finished or out of it, physically or mentally exhausted, overwhelmed, or in a state of complete ruin. While "TAXED" focuses on the burden or pressure you're feeling, the weight of a challenging or draining situation, especially in stress or responsibility...So yeah, not the same.

Just try to remember how you feel after an all-nighter or a week of back-to-back exams: you're just TAXED, physically and mentally. It's like all your energy's been taken from you (taxed, get it?), leaving you struggling to get through.

You'll hear it in contexts like, "MAN, AFTER THAT SHIFT, I'M SO TAXED," or "I CAN'T DO ANYTHING ELSE TODAY; I'M TAXED." Essentially, you're so done that even thinking about doing anything extra is just not happening. TAXED can also apply to situations, not just people. Like, you could say, "THIS WEEK HAS BEEN TAXED," to mean it's been relentless and exhausting.

If you find yourself taxed? It's time to recharge, drink some water, or maybe TOUCH GRASS (Gen Z's favorite remedy for internet burnout). Remember, TAXED isn't just tired; it's tired on another level, like you've been running on fumes for way too long. Take a nap, and then take another one, because Gen Z says you've earned it. Oldie...

TEA

Why did the Gen Zer paint their room hashtag blue? Because life's better in #0000FF. By now, you should be able to decode this joke. If not, please make yourself some tea and read the book all over again. (No, I am serious.)

Anyways, where was I? Ah yes. The TEA.

If you hear someone drop this term, grab your cup, because things are about to get juicy. TEA is all about the gossip, the latest news, the scandalous stories, the dirt—the kind of info that makes you sit up and go, "WAIT, WHAT?" It's that moment when you're told something so wild or intriguing that you can't help but sip it in like it's a piping hot beverage.

The phrase "SPILL THE TEA" is the go-to expression when someone wants you to share the juicy details of a story or gossip. For example, if your friend walks in and you're like, "GIRL, I HAVE THE TEA," they know you're about to drop some hot gossip. It's like you've just come back from the gossip mines with a golden nugget of information, and now everyone's waiting for you to spill.

But here's the thing about TEA: it's not just about any boring ol' info—it's about the GOOD stuff. If you're talking about someone's love life, a juicy fight, or a shady situation, that's where the real tea comes in. "YOU WON'T BELIEVE WHAT I HEARD—TEA LEVEL: BOILING." And, yes, TEA is often used as a euphemism for drama. That friend who always seems to know EVERYTHING? They've probably got the tea on lock.

Of course, while it's fun to spill the tea, it's even better when you're the one getting the TEA spilled on you. Get ready for a front-row seat to all the drama, but don't forget: with great tea comes great responsibility. Share wisely, because not everyone needs to know how much you REALLY know about their life. Unless, of course, you just want to sip your tea and watch the chaos unfold. "OH, I'M JUST HERE FOR THE TEA."

THOT

Proceed only if you are above the age of...uhm...maturity? Well, anyway, you want to know about THOT, huh? Alright, brace yourself—because this one's a little spicy, and if you're just learning it now, well...bless your heart.

THOT stands for "THAT HO OVER THERE." Yep, you read that right. It's basically Gen Z's way of calling someone out for being a little too thirsty for attention, usually in the romantic (or let's be real, physical) department. If someone's being extra flirty, posting a few too many selfies in the same day, or just...well, letting everyone know they're available, then—bam, they're labeled a THOT. You might see people use it like, "She's acting like such a THOT right now," or just "THOT BEHAVIOR" when someone is living their best "I'm here to be noticed" life.

And don't get it twisted, this isn't always a bad thing. Sure, being called a THOT is kind of a roast, but it's also an acknowledgement that someone is rocking their confidence and shooting their shot—even if it's a little TOO obvious. We're in the age of thirst traps, after all, and if you're out there posting one gym selfie after another, it's pretty clear you're angling for those likes. And, let's be honest, we're all THOT material on occasion.

Before you get high and mighty, take a look at your own posts. You know that perfectly filtered beach pic from your last vacation? Or that mirror selfie with just the right lighting? Yeah, you knew exactly what you were doing, THOT.

Touch grass

Tired of reading this book? Why don't you set it aside and touch some grass? Yep, that's exactly NOT what 'touch grass' means. It's actually a bit mean, very mean slang. (Not really, but somehow Gen Z peeps got offended when I told them that.)

TOUCH GRASS—a perfect blend of shade, advice, and a little reality check all in one.(Yup, that is why a lot get offended.) If someone tells you to TOUCH GRASS, it's their polite (or not-so-polite) way of saying, "Get off the internet, go outside, and maybe...reconnect with reality." Basically, they're suggesting that you might be a little too deep in your online world, and it's time to step away from the screen and rejoin the real world.

TOUCH GRASS usually comes out when someone's getting way too worked up over something trivial, like a heated argument about which fictional character could beat up another. Or maybe they're diving too deep into a rabbit hole, blowing up over a minor point that only exists online. That's when someone comes in with the "BRO, TOUCH GRASS." Translation: go outside, breathe in some fresh air, maybe let go of whatever weird internet beef you've created. It's a reminder that there's a world beyond the keyboard and that sometimes, yes, you really do need a break.

And let's be real, we could all use a little TOUCHING GRASS moment now and then.(I am definitely going to TOUCH GRASS after I finish this slang chapter.) And if someone tells you to TOUCH GRASS, don't get too offended. Just remember that it's probably time to close out of those fifty-five tabs, put your phone down, and maybe—just maybe—see what the sun actually looks like. (Wear glasses, sunglasses.)

Tweaking

"Tweaking" is like the little sibling of DELULU—they mean different things, yet kinda the same, but still different. And yet...the same, and still different. Alright, I'm tweaking here...

If someone says you're TWEAKING, it's not exactly a compliment. In Gen Z slang, TWEAKING means you're acting irrational, over-the-top, or just flat-out weird about something. Maybe you're blowing a small problem way out of proportion, or you're wildly overreacting to something minor. Someone might throw a "BRUH, YOU'RE TWEAKING" your way to let you know you need to chill out, take a step back, and maybe reconsider how you're acting.

Imagine you're in a group chat, and someone gets overly dramatic about a tiny disagreement, sending a 20-message rant that nobody asked for. Or maybe you see someone freaking out because they're convinced their favorite celebrity looked at them in their IG story (no, that's not proof they know you exist). Both of these situations? Definitely TWEAKING.

Gen Z is all about keeping it real, so if you're called out for TWEAKING, it's basically someone saying you need to get a grip. It's the modern equivalent of "take a chill pill" or "relax." But, if you want to be a bit too extra, expect a "YOU'RE TWEAKING" and try not to take it personally. It's just the Gen Z way of saying, "HEY, BREATHE. IT'S REALLY NOT THAT DEEP."

Unsmart.

Do you really need a word to know yourself? Oh, did I just call you unsmart? Yes, I did. Otherwise, why would you buy this piece of wrecked literature?

(Look, you've gotten so far into my book; it's time you realize I like teasing my readers with offensive humor. So if it makes you mad and frustrated, buy another copy and give it to your enemy. Or better yet, give it to your best friend.)

Ok, where were we? Oh yes, UNSMART.

Here's the thing, "unsmart" is just the Gen Z way of saying someone's lacking in the intelligence department. Imagine you're the opposite of Einstein (which, judging by how long it took you to get this far, might not be hard to imagine. I am watching you). You say or do something UNSMART, and voilà, you've nailed it. It's the ultimate (just kidding, not overusing that word for your sake) word to gently roast someone who's not quite firing on all intellectual cylinders.

When someone does something so UNSMART you're left staring at them in disbelief, it's that moment of UNSMARTNESS that really seals the deal. Did they microwave metal? UNSMART. Forget to check if the Wi-Fi is on while complaining about "the internet being down"? UNSMART. And if they call a meme A ME-ME, well, congratulations, you've just witnessed the definition of UNSMART.

But, if you're getting called unsmart, take it as a little nudge. It's like saying, "Hey, you're being a little slow on the uptake here." Or maybe even, "Bless your heart, your brain could use a software update." You know, like the one you're probably missing out on by not reading more books—say, for example, this one? (Just kidding. My book grants 100% of smart.)

But in all honesty, UNSMART is a useful tool. It's the ultimate subtle shade, like a verbal eye-roll for moments that are too ridiculous to ignore. Next time you encounter someone making a LOWKEY questionable choice, just hit them with a gentle, "Not your smartest moment, huh?" Or even better: just smile, shake your head, and say, "UNSMART."

UWU

No, just no.

I'm going to skip this one.

Every time I hear Gen Z girls say it, I feel a sudden urge to... slap a baby rabbit, and let's just say it's an intense feeling. But (sigh) I must do my job as a (not very) professional author and educator, and explain the meaning of UWU...

UWU is basically an online way of expressing a super adorable, mushy, over-the-top level of cuteness. Imagine a cartoonishly cute face—little round eyes, soft cheeks, a tiny mouth—all rolled into three letters. UWU is the kind of word you might use if you're trying to act innocent or sweet, and it's got a hint of playful, wholesome energy to it. Think "puppy eyes" or "tiny kitten purr," and you've got the right vibe. (And yes, some—but not all—Gen Z girls do it to act cutesy.)

You might see people drop an UWU in a text or comment when they're feeling soft or if they're trying to be extra cute. If someone sends you a compliment and you respond with UWU, it's like blushing in text form. "YOU LOOK SO CUTE TODAY! UWU"—it's all about the warm fuzzies.

But be warned: UWU is polarizing. People either love it or they think it's the cringe equivalent of a glittery MySpace profile. So, use it wisely. Or don't. I mean, if you're going for that ultra-sweet, slightly ironic internet cuteness, go full UWU and don't look back. Just be prepared for someone to lovingly (or not-so-lovingly) roast you for it.

VIBE and Vibe Check

VIBE and VIBE CHECK. These aren't just words; they're practically a lifestyle at this point. Remember them—and remember them well.

So, let's break it down for you in a way your "big brain" can handle.

First, VIBE. This is Gen Z's all-encompassing term for energy, mood, or the "aura" someone (or something) is putting out. Like, "Are you a good vibe?" or "This place has bad vibes." It's that gut feeling, that certain je ne sais quoi. Basically, if you don't know what a vibe is, there's a good chance you've been putting out the wrong one this whole time. Ouch.

If you're "vibing," you're in the zone, basking in pure, undisturbed good energy. It's like being in that perfect state of chill where everything feels just right. Think of it as the ultimate level of relaxation mixed with "I'm too cool to be bothered right now." You might be listening to music, hanging out with friends, or even just spacing out, but you're totally feeling yourself in the best way possible.

Second, VIBE CHECK. Imagine you're just minding your own business, thinking you're cool, and suddenly someone hits you with a vibe check. It's a way of asking, "Are you still bringing the right energy, or have you veered into Unsmooth, Uncool, and, dare I say, Unsmart territory?" If you pass the vibe check, congrats, you're vibing just fine. If you fail, well... let's just say you might want to rethink your life choices.

Here's a little hint: (A free one at that) if you have to ask, "What's a vibe?" there's a good chance you might not be in sync with one right now. But hey, we all have our off days. Just try to pick up on the vibe next time before you end up killing it.So there it is, two words that separate those who are effortlessly cool from those who... maybe aren't.

Wig

You've stepped into WIG now! Look at you, leveling up your slang game to the end. We're almost there, my friend—you'll soon be free of this book...and me.

(I'll miss you—but mostly, I'll miss your money. Hey, I may be an a$$hole, but at least I'm an honest one.)

WIG is one of those terms that can hit like a lightning bolt of shock, awe, and admiration—basically the Gen Z way of saying, "I"m absolutely floored right now." It's what you drop when something is so unexpectedly impressive that it metaphorically snatches your wig right off your head and sends it flying into another dimension. This isn't just "cool"; it's SHOCK AND AWE in two syllables.

When you hear someone gasp and say "WIG," they're experiencing a moment so powerful it feels like an out-of-body experience. It's like if you were to see your favorite celebrity walk by and all you can do is scream "WIG" as you clutch your head because nothing else can contain your excitement. And if you're the one making people say "WIG," congratulations— you've achieved peak fabulousness.

Example, since you'll probably need it to fully grasp this majestic concept: Imagine you're watching your friend hit every note of their favorite Beyoncé song in a karaoke bar. They're SLAYING it, and you're sitting there, gobsmacked. The only appropriate reaction is to mouth, "WIG," as you gesture helplessly to the imaginary hair on your head that's just been blown right off.

And don't get it twisted—WIG is reserved for moments that are so powerful they defy normal reactions. Your friend ordering a coffee? Not WIG. Your friend walking in with a glow-up so intense it blinds you on the spot? WIG.

If you're still confused, maybe you should just experience it for real—try looking up a killer dance routine or a plot twist you DIDN'T see coming. If you feel that sudden urge to gasp and clutch your imaginary wig, you're getting it. And if you still don't feel anything, maybe you're just missing that spark that Gen Z has naturally. (Not my fault, by the way.)

Next time something blows your mind, make sure to yell WIG! And if people look at you like you're nuts? Well, they're clearly not in on the fabulous secret, are they?

YAAS

You've hit a gold mine, my friend.

This is the peak of exaggerated excitement, praise, and all-around hype. YAAAAAASSSSSSSSS, BABAEY.

YAAS is the verbal equivalent of throwing a confetti cannon at someone, blasting them with love and enthusiasm. You know when something is so good, so perfect, that "yes" just won't cut it anymore? You need YAAS, with that extra, drawn-out flair. It's like the world's biggest "YAAAASSSSSS" from a drag queen who just nailed a high-kick routine and is NOT holding back.

When you hear someone drop a big YAAS, you know they are absolutely LIVING for whatever just happened. It's the hype you give when your friend posts a picture that slaps, when your crush finally texts back, or when you land the perfect comeback in an argument you were definitely losing five minutes ago. It's the ultimate YES, but with extra glitter and sparkle. Because why settle for regular enthusiasm when you can have a full-on celebration?

Your friend shows up wearing an outfit so on-point, so FLAWLESS, it could make even the dullest moment feel like a runway show. You gasp and scream, "YAASSSSS," because there is no other word that could possibly convey how deeply impressed you are.

And don't forget—YAAS is EXTRA. YAAAAASSS is super EXTRA. ("Extra" is also EXTRA, but you get my point.) It's meant to be loud. It's meant to be dramatic. And it's the perfect way to show someone you are 100% here for their existence, their choices, their vibe—whether they're wearing the most questionable pair of shoes or just sent you a meme that made your soul laugh. YAAS can even turn a simple "good job" into an iconic moment. "YAASSSS queen, you nailed it!" (Because yes, you're calling them royalty now. You get an extra point for understanding that.)

If you DON'T use YAAS in your daily life, well, that's a crime and you should be in jail. And if you're still asking what it means, I'm wondering how you're still functioning as a human being in 20xx or whenever year you are reading this book. Catch up, bud. The YAAS train is pulling out, and you need to get on board.

So, there it is. The ULTIMATE enthusiasm.

The YAAS.

Let's just hope you use it in context, or your friends will be YAPPING about how out-of-touch you are next. (But hey, at least you'll know how to handle it with a YAAS, right?)

YAP

YAP isn't exactly Gen Z slang, per se, but they still use it here and there. You probably know what it means, but if you don't—well, damn, I'm glad you decided to buy this book (or accept it as a gift). Buckle up, because we're diving deeper into this one—whether you're ready or not.

"Yap" is what WE/THEY (as in, us old farts and them Gen Z peeps) use to describe someone who just can't stop running their mouth. And when I say "can't stop," I mean it's like they've activated a non-stop verbal machine with no off button. They're just going on and on, spewing out everything from their latest online shopping haul to their in-depth analysis of their friend's "questionable" haircut. Basically, if someone's YAPPING, you're mentally trying to escape, but it's like being stuck in a never-ending loop of nonsense.

And let's be real here, if you're the one YAPPING, you probably have no clue how much you're annoying everyone around you. It's like watching someone chew loudly in your ear without realizing you can hear every single bite. But don't worry—YAP is also a great way to describe that annoying, persistent chatter that you can't escape. It's like they're trying to fill the silence, but the only thing they're really filling is the air with pointless noise.

Free example time, since I know you need it: You're trying to watch a movie, and your friend is sitting next to you, talking about their day, their cousin's dog, and how they accidentally fell asleep in a yoga class—FOR THE FIFTH TIME this week. You turn to them, exhausted, and go, "Can you stop yapping for five seconds? I'm trying to actually enjoy this movie."

However, YAP doesn't always need to be negative. You could be saying something sarcastic, like when someone's going on about how "super busy" they are at work. "Oh, YAP about it some more, Karen. We get it, your life is a whirlwind." You're not DIRECTLY telling them to shut up, but you're definitely making it clear you're done hearing about it.

Here's the thing: YAP is versatile. It can be playful, like when you're teasing a friend who can't seem to stop talking about their DEEP thoughts on the latest TikTok trend. Or it can be more pointed, like when you're at a party, and someone's loudly blabbering about their podcast "that you REALLY should check out" but you have no interest. "Yap" is the weapon of choice for handling those kinds of moments without breaking a sweat.

Oh shoot, I just realized...

I've been YAPPING this whole time...

Sorry...

YEET

You may have heard the expression "YEET THE CHILD."

Now, now—before you call the police, FBI, or Child Protective Services, let me explain. It does not mean, in any way, to throw a child against the wall. It's slang for throwing something with force and without regard for the object being tossed. (Which is exactly why they dropped "child" part of the slang and just stuck with "YEET")

Now, if you already know what YEET means, good for you, time traveler. But if you don't, you're either a thousand years old, unsmart, or just a hopeless case (I'm betting on the latter). Let me educate you so you can at least ATTEMPT to keep up with Gen Z for once.

"Yeet" is the expression of throwing something with intense enthusiasm, passion, or reckless abandon. It's not just about tossing; it's about yeeting — a wild, dramatic hurl that may or may not involve knowing where the object will land. You don't just yeet something lightly; if you're not risking a broken vase or an insulted friend, are you really yeeting?

Example time, since I know you need the help: you see an empty soda can and yeet it across the room with absolutely no concern for where it lands. It could go in the trash, or it could smack your friend right in the face. Either way, it's about the ENERGY.

And yes, you can even yeet yourself—into a pile of snow, off a couch, or into a questionable life choice. "Yeet!" you declare, and off you go, with no plan or sense of dignity.

There, did that sink in? Or do I need to YEET myself out of here because you're just too far gone?

YEET myself

Yummers.

Look at you, making it to the end of the book, trying to keep up with Gen Z slang like you've got a chance. Props to you, old pal. Now, let me reward you with an explanation of this word.

"Yummers" is a silly, exaggerated way of saying something is delicious, tasty, or straight-up delightful. It's like saying "yum," but with so much extra enthusiasm you might just pop a vein. Imagine the kind of "yum" you'd yell when devouring an entire pizza by yourself at midnight with no shame—THAT'S yummers.

Let say you're chowing down on some fries, double-dipping into ketchup, and maybe even RANCH because you're living on the edge. You take a bite and, in pure, unfettered bliss, say, "Yummers!"

Congratulations, you've officially embraced the zest of Gen Z…or at least given it your best attempt.

And hey, if you overuse it and annoy everyone around you? Extra points. Gen Z would probably be proud. I am proud.

GEN Z LINGO TEST.

Now, you've finally finished my book.

Congrats!

To earn your Understanding Gen Z Slang certification, you must answer the 25 questions below.

Once you complete them, you'll officially know all of the Gen Z slangs.

1. What word describes someone who is honest and genuine, especially when expressing bold opinions?

2. What term would you use to describe someone who's obsessed with trends and lacks originality?

3. What's the go-to word to express exasperation or disbelief?

4. What word describes someone or something that seems suspicious or shady?

5. What term refers to someone who is excessively devoted to pleasing or supporting someone they're interested in?

6. What word describes a confident, lone-wolf personality that thrives without social validation?

7. What phrase might Gen Z use to humorously dismiss an out-of-touch opinion? (OLD PEEPS)

8. What's the slang term for someone who's entertaining a wildly unrealistic fantasy or scenario?

9. What word would you use if you think someone's lying?

10. What slang term describes a super-confident guy who's also popular and often stereotypically attractive?

11. What term is used to praise someone's incredible performance or success?

12. What's the Gen Z slang for someone's outfit?

13. What word describes someone or something that's super popular and exciting?

14. What term would you use to describe someone who seems robotic, following scripts like an extra in a video game?

15. What word describes someone who's over-the-top dramatic or doing more than necessary?

16. What term is used for a person who's entitled, demanding, and often complains to get what they want?

17. What is the enthusiastic Gen Z way to say "yes!" or show excitement?

18. What word describes someone who's bitter or upset, especially over something minor?

19. What word is used for a meme that's really funny, often in an edgy or bizarre way?

20. What term would you use to describe something awkward, embarrassing, or socially off?

21. What word describes something that's average, unremarkable, or just okay?

22. What state has become a Gen Z meme symbolizing absurdity or strangeness?

23. What term describes someone who seeks validation by trying to make themselves look better than others?

24. What word do you use to refer to gossip or juicy news?

25. What phrase would you use to emphasize you're telling the truth?

ANSWERS

1. Answer: Based
2. Answer: Basic
3. Answer: Bruh
4. Answer: Sus
5. Answer: Simp
6. Answer: Sigma
7. Answer: OK Boomer
8. Answer: Delulu
9. Answer: Cap
10. Answer: Chad
11. Answer: Cook
12. Answer: Fit
13. Answer: Hype
14. Answer: NPC
15. Answer: Extra
16. Answer: Karen
17. Answer: YAAS
18. Answer: Salty
19. Answer: Dank
20. Answer: Cringe
21. Answer: Mid
22. Answer: Ohio
23. Answer: Pick me
24. Answer: Tea
25. Answer: No cap

Author's Notes.

Hey, I've gotta say, I'm ridiculously proud of you for actually finishing UNDERSTANDING GEN Z SLANG.

I mean, who knew you could pull your eyes away from TV or newspaper for long enough to flip through a whole book? But seriously, you're the real MVP for taking the time to read it. You've officially leveled up from a "lowkey reader" to an ACTUAL BOOK BASED SIGMA FINISHER.

I joke a lot, but big props to you for sticking with the book. Don't let it go to your head now, but you might just be one of the few Gen Z'ers who can survive in a world without 3-second attention spans.

Take that certificate of recognition and show it to all of your friends that you actually understand the Gen Z slangs.

You are BASED SIGMA CHAD.

Proud of you, for real!

Certificate of Recognition

Presented to _____

For really vibing with Gen Z and getting the whole deal by finishing UNDERSTANDING GEN Z SLANGS.

You are truly SIGMA and Forklift Certified.

Z

Your SIMPING to enhance your BASED knowledge and fostering generational understanding actually SLAPS and appreciated.

Date: _____

[Signature]_____

Emily T. Jacobs.

Author, GEN Z Learner, Mother of eleven, and Dedicated Internet Troll.

Printed in Great Britain
by Amazon